To Set Them Free

THE EARLY YEARS OF

MUSTAFA KEMAL ATATÜRK

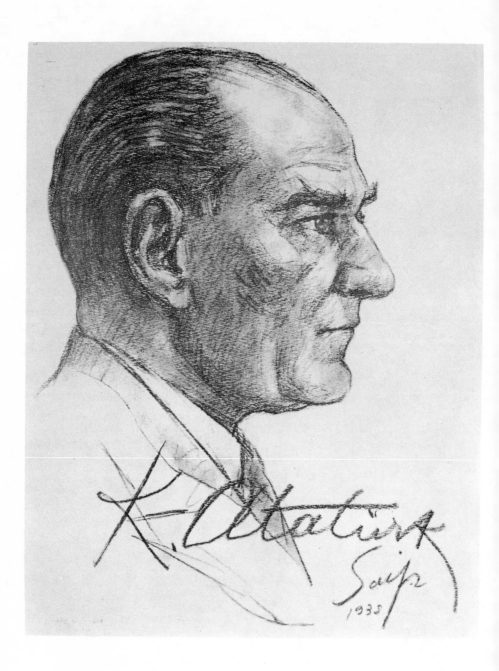

To Set Them Free

The Early Years
of Mustafa Kemal Atatürk

BARBARA K. WALKER
FILIZ EROL
MINE EROL

TOMPSON & RUTTER INC
Grantham, New Hampshire

Library of Congress Cataloging in Publication Data

Walker, Barbara K
   To set them free.

   SUMMARY: A biography of the first President of
the Turkish Republic which emphasizes his childhood
and early military career.
      1. Atatürk, Kamâl, Pres. Turkey, d. 1938.
      2. Turkey—Presidents—Biography.
       [1. Atatürk, Kamâl, Pres. Turkey, d. 1938.
      2. Turkey—Presidents]
     I. Erol, Filiz, joint author.
    II. Erol, Mine, joint author.
   III. Title
DR592.K4W34   956.1'024'0924   [B]   [92]   80–21127

ISBN 0-936988-00-2 (cloth)
ISBN 0-936988-02-9 (paper)

First published in 1981, the hundredth
anniversary of the birth of Mustafa
Kemal Atatürk, by Tompson & Rutter Inc
of Grantham, New Hampshire 03753

There are two Mustafa Kemals. One is I, the mortal Mustafa Kemal; the other is the Mustafa Kemal who has been created by the Turkish people. I represent that man.

What if I did happen to appear at a particular moment in time, when the existence of our nation was in danger? Wasn't it a Turkish mother who gave birth to me? Will not Turkish mothers bear more Mustafa Kemals? The credit is the nation's, not mine.

(Quotation from Enver Ziya Karal, *Atatürk'ten Düşünceler*)
[p. 133. Ankara: Türk Tarih Kurumu Basımevi, 1956.]

CONTENTS

PREFACE

THE STORY OF Mustafa Kemal Atatürk as a man has long attracted the interest of readers and writers alike, both inside Turkey and beyond her borders. But a relatively complete story of this great Turkish leader's boyhood and youth has never been made available to those outside his own land, and in very fragmentary form even to the Turks themselves. The closest attempt to acquaint readers in Turkey with the boyhood and youth of Atatürk has been the fine *Babamız Atatürk* [Our Father Atatürk], written by Falih Rıfkı Atay. Even this account devotes only a small fraction of its space to his early years. Why is this so? In the first place, readers have been concerned largely with the *mature* Atatürk because of the remarkable changes he accomplished in his country. In the second place, Atatürk's achievements have made it

9

seem almost unthinkable that he could ever have been a *child* at all; to imagine this great hero engaged in childlike activities seems almost an impertinence. In the third place, information on his childhood and youth is available only in bits and pieces, scattered among many sources, and each piece appears in almost direct contradiction with one or more of the others.

In 1961, Filiz Erol, Mine Erol, and I decided to work together to present to American and Turkish readers the fullest possible account of the growing years of Atatürk, since we believed that Atatürk the man was clearly visible in those early years. We divided the work in this way: Mine Erol, of the History Department at Ankara University, would collect all the manuscripts, pamphlets, newspapers, books, and other historical and biographical sources in Turkish that she could find. Filiz Erol, of the English Department at Ankara University, would make a literal translation into English of all these materials; I would translate those that were found in other languages. Then I would select from this treasury, checking against all available written and oral sources, those incidents and details which could be confirmed by at least two reasonably objective scholarly avenues of information — incidents that could be both defended and documented — and combine and shape them into a readable and dependable study of Atatürk's early years. Also, since Atatürk's youthful years hold their special significance because of those things which he accomplished as a man, I would be responsible for summarizing in a final chapter, an Afterword, the events and achievements of Atatürk's mature years, materials which had provided the substance for countless books over a number of decades. This book — *To Set Them Free: The Early Years of Mustafa Kemal Atatürk* — is the result of our twenty years of teamwork. It must be noted that all of the dialogue furnished in this account has been exposed to the same tests of validity as have the statements of fact included; where we have credited historical figures with remarks which are not known to be their actual words, we have been reassured that such remarks are true to their acknowledged sentiments. As nearly as is humanly possible, we have presented the young Atatürk as he was known to his family and to his contemporaries and as he can honestly and fairly be known by people the world over.

In addition to the hundreds of newspaper accounts, manuscripts, pamphlets, and books in Turkish, French, German, and English that we read, we located and interviewed all those men and women still living who had known Atatürk in his earlier years or had made special studies of his life. Many of the people whom we interviewed, especially during the summer of 1966, were old and are now — at the hundredth anniversary of Atatürk's birth — no longer alive; the tape recordings of these interviews and/or written transcriptions of the interviews, however, have been preserved in the Archive of Turkish Oral Narrative, housed in the Texas Tech University Library, Lubbock, Texas. We were fortunate indeed to reach those individuals at the time we did. Others of our informants have survived to taste the sweetness of this celebration. To them, long life! We wish to thank especially Bayan Nimet Arsal, Falih Rıfkı Atay, Dr. Afet Inan, Enver Ziya Karal, Müdür Ziya Onaran (of the Türk Inkilap Müsesi in Ankara), and Enver Behnan Şapolyo for oral information which assisted us in the completion of our work. We are indebted also to Dr. Metin Tamkoç, political scientist, and to Bayan Günseli Tamkoç, sociologist, for their reading and criticism of the manuscript.

Words are inadequate to express our appreciation to Barbara L. Geyer for her preparation of the map for this study. Our cartographer's source for the outlines of

11

the land areas was *Citizens Atlas of the World* (John Bartholomew, 1952) and for the 1900 national boundaries was Muir's *Historical Atlas, Ancient and Modern,* 6th ed., R. F. Treharne and H. Fullard, editors (George Philip & Son, 1976); Petermann's [Geographische] *Mitteilungen,* Volume 59, Tafel 22 (1913), and Volume 66, Tafel 31 (1920), also proved invaluable in this work. Miss Geyer herself is indebted — as are we — to Dr. Gary Elbow, Associate Professor, Department of Geography, Texas Tech University, for the identification of several sites in a Library of Congress source published in 1917 by Service Topographique des Armées D'Orient [France], Salonique and Verria sheets. Spellings of place names varied widely; as nearly as possible, they conform to those used in the text.

The charcoal sketch of Atatürk used as a frontispiece was drawn by Saip Tuna; it has been widely distributed in Turkey in postcard form and has been reproduced on a Turkish postage stamp. The sketch was furnished by Prof. Ahmet F. Uysal, a friend of the artist and of the authors.

The photographs that illustrate this book are accepted in Turkey as accurate reflections of Atatürk and his surroundings. The best mirror of Atatürk, however, still lies in the lives of the Turks, whom he set free from the iron rule of the Ottoman Empire, the impositions of other nations, and the shackles of the past.

Lubbock, Texas　　　　　　　　　BARBARA K. WALKER, *Curator*
Archive of Turkish Oral Narrative
Texas Tech University

1

The First Six Years

Tok, tok, tok! There was a noisy knocking on the heavy front door. "May it be good news!" murmured the old woman. She adjusted her head scarf to cover her face and then hurried to answer.

On the doorstep stood small Ömer, the second son of Ali Riza and Zübeyde, the old woman's neighbors in the hilly Moslem quarter of Salonica overlooking the Aegean Sea. "Come quickly!" he urged. "I have a new brother! Hatice Kadın (*kadın* means "woman" or "matron"), the midwife, is still there. And the *hoca* (Moslem preacher and teacher) is coming, too!"

Hastily putting on her *çarşaf* (long black cape covering the head and face), the old woman hurried into the street with Ömer. Like the rest of the neighbors in that close community, she had eagerly awaited the news of the child's birth. Now they all knew: Ömer had a new brother. That made three fine boys to share the pittance Ali Riza made each month from his lumber business. Well, Allah (God) knew best . . .

In a moment the neighbor had come into the mother's bedroom, with its cozy fireplace warm, but its windows open to the spring air. "Look! There is the *hoca* now," said Ömer. "What is he doing to my brother?"

The *hoca*, his turban nodding as he leaned forward, bent to the ear of the new baby. "Mustafa," he whispered. And thus, according to the Moslem custom, the baby was given the name that the child's father had chosen for him.

Raising his head again, the *hoca* smiled at the baby's father, Ali Riza. "Ali Riza Bey" (*Bey* is a title of respect; there were no family names in those days), he said, "you have a fine, strong son in Mustafa. May he live long!" And to ward off the evil eye, he fingered a blue bead on his wide belt (protection against loss of good fortune when praise was given).

Ali Riza looked at his new son, a fair-haired child with clear blue eyes like his mother Zübeyde's. What father would not be proud of such a boy? Still, he sighed. This child had come into a troubled family in a troubled time. Allah alone could oversee his growing.

The father looked above the baby's head at a fine curved sword, a souvenir of his own proud service in 1876 in the Sultan's army. If Mustafa chose, he could make his way as a soldier. That was a man's route, the soldier's way.

At one side, the mother, Zübeyde, saw her husband look at the sword. She glanced quickly at the baby as she read her husband's thought. Then she looked intently at the *hoca*, a wise, learned man. *There* was the proper future for her new son, a life as a *hoca*, a holy man. Her eyes returned to her husband. Yes, she would meet

14

opposition from Ali Riza. But she would have her way, nonetheless.

Thus on that spring day of 1881 in Salonica in this plain setting was born a boy who one day would save his country from its enemies on all sides, within and without — a boy destined for greatness as a soldier-statesman, Mustafa Kemal Atatürk.

And what of Salonica? Was it a good place for a boy to be born, to grow up? Through the open window came the babble and stir of a busy city, a crowded city, a city into whose harbor came ships from many lands. Salonica sprawled across the hills which came down almost to the water's edge, a city known for its trade and for its many nations and ethnic groups, each settled in its own sector or quarter — Spanish, Greeks, Jews, Albanians, Macedonians, French, Turks — a melting pot of the far-flung Ottoman Empire. Here a boy could come to know the complexity of the world, to test himself against the challenge of his times.

Suddenly the baby cried, a hungry cry, a strong cry. Taking the baby aside, Zübeyde nursed him. All the care and love a mother could spend would be given to this baby, her third son, her Mustafa. Caught up in tenderness for her small son, Zübeyde no longer heard the chatter in the room, man talk, talk between the *hoca* and her husband, one curious always to learn about this world in which he played such a tiny part.

Himself a Turk born in Monastır (some sources say Salonica), the son of a soldier named Ahmet and the nephew of an elementary-school teacher called Mehmet, Ali Riza had been for years an ill-paid clerk in the Customs Administration of the Turkish government. His three gold liras a month could barely stretch to feed and clothe his family and to maintain their house, a substantial pink-colored three-story frame building on Koca Kasımpaşa, in the Ahmet Subaşı quarter (a Moslem

15

sector also called Hatuniye) close to an orphanage school, Sanayı Okulu. At last, pressed financially, he had retired from his government post and had gone into the lumber trade in partnership with Cafer Efendi (*Efendi* is a title of respect), a trade constantly threatened by the activities of bandits in the forested areas from which Ali Riza had to secure the lumber for their business. Among all his associates, Ali Riza was known as a poor but honorable man, with minimal formal education but with a thirst to learn and to understand the workings of the Ottoman Empire and of the larger world of which it was a part. His own eagerness to learn prompted his interest in the new private schools being opened in various parts of Salonica by educated men — schools patterned after those in Europe and in America, schools that he felt would provide the best possible training for boys growing up in a rapidly changing and Westernizing world.

Zübeyde, Mustafa's mother, who was nearly twenty years younger than her husband, was a Macedonian of highly respected parents. Her father, Ahmet Ibrahim, had been a prosperous landholder and cattle raiser in Langaza, twenty miles northeast of Salonica. When Zübeyde, the only daughter, was fourteen, her family had moved to Salonica — some sources say her father decided on the move to Salonica in order to ensure the best possible medical care for his daughter. Like most women of that time, Zübeyde had had no formal education, but she was clever and alert, and vitally concerned about the opportunities available to her children. She was considered beautiful, with high cheekbones, widely spaced blue-gray eyes, and a firm chin. As was customary for Moslem women of her time, she was married at an early age, and was barely twenty years old at the time her son Mustafa was born. Throughout Mustafa's youth, Zübeyde held a dream for him, a dream that was to be far exceeded by what actually came to pass. A devout Moslem, she stoutly supported the traditional religious schools taught by *hocas* for the purpose of training young Moslems for devout and useful lives. Her Mustafa, she thought, should one day be a teacher himself, a revered *hoca*. But during Mustafa's early years she kept these thoughts to herself, content to see him growing strong and healthy.

In keeping with custom, Mustafa was nursed by several "milk mothers" in addition to his own mother, Zübeyde. By nursing someone else's child, a milk mother (like a godmother in other cultures) proved her interest in him and her continuing concern for his welfare. First and most significant among these milk mothers of Mustafa was Ümmügül Molla, but also included were other women — some Moslem, some Christian — who were attracted by the forthright, approachable child with his open manner and direct gaze. During Mustafa's earliest years, then, he had the care and interest of a number of women, including his mother's black servant Üftade and his own nursemaid, a Macedonian woman, who tended him from day to day and sang to him the traditional folksongs of her people.

It was a comfortable, safe place for a small boy to grow, despite the scant amount of money that Ali Riza was able to bring home from his work as a lumber merchant. Mustafa had two brothers, Ahmet and Ömer, who delighted to play with him. Ahmet had been seven years old when Mustafa was born, and Ömer six. Their mother, Zübeyde, spent all her time and her attention on her three boys. And Ali Riza was a tender and loving father.

There was a grandmother, too. Zübeyde's mother, Ayşe, lived not far from Salonica at Rapla, on a farm managed for its wealthy Salonica owner by her son Hüseyin. From that farm each time the grandmother

17

visited, there would be pots of delicious yoghurt and fresh cheese and milk and eggs and meat. Like most grandmothers, this one had a great deal of time for talking with her grandsons, and for telling them stories, not only marvelous tales of genies and monsters and enchanted animals, but exciting tales of things that had happened in their own family.

As Mustafa grew in size, he began to play more with his brothers. The large upstairs bay windows overlooking the busy street were a favorite play place; so were the balcony in the back, overlooking the garden and the trees — alive with birds — and the garden itself, with its sweet-smelling honeysuckle and roses and its ferns and vervain and portulacas. There in the garden were insects to trap, and lizards to poke and prod as they scuttled among the grass and moss. It was a good life for a curious, thoughtful boy.

To this snug house in 1883 came sudden and unexpected trouble. One morning Mustafa, who was not quite two, wanted Ömer to get up out of bed and play. But Ömer refused. "Go call Mother," he said. "My throat hurts, and I can't call her." Mustafa stared at his brother. Then, still wanting to play, he went over to Ahmet's bed. Ahmet lay there, his eyes big with fever. He shook his head slowly as Mustafa said, "Play?"

Mustafa began to cry. He could not understand why his brothers were behaving so strangely. "Mother, Mother!" he called, running to the kitchen. "Come see!"

Zübeyde sensed the panic in Mustafa's voice and came running. There lay Ahmet and Ömer, flushed with fever. She laid cool cloths on their foreheads to make them more comfortable, and then she sent the maid to fetch the best doctor she could find, Dr. Jak, a man well along in years.

It was several hours before the doctor could come. But he knew almost before he came what the illness was.

He had seen all too many cases of it these past few days in the crowded city. It was the dreaded diphtheria, for which nothing at all could be done. In those times, doctors could do very little to help people who were seriously ill. Those who were meant to die died, and those who were meant to live lived, all according to the will of holy Allah.

In three days, it was all over. Ömer and Ahmet were washed and wrapped for burial, and the house, which had rung with the shouts of three active boys, echoed to Mustafa's calling. "Ahmet! Ömer!" Little Mustafa could not understand that his brothers would never play with him again.

Ali Riza and Zübeyde grieved for their two sons, as they had grieved seven years earlier for a daughter, Fatma. But all the while, their wonder grew: how had Mustafa escaped the dreadful disease? He had slept in the same room with Ahmet and Ömer, had played constantly with them, had even drunk from the same glass. Allah be praised, he had been spared from diphtheria. Their one boy was strong and healthy and handsome. From this time, Mustafa became ever dearer to his parents. They took great interest and great pride in whatever he said and did. And Mustafa was always busy, always asking questions, learning about the things and the people around him.

One day when Mustafa was four there was a great stir of excitement in the house. A little girl, Makbule, was born to Zübeyde. At last there would be someone for Mustafa to play with! But of course the baby was too small now to do anything but cry and eat and sleep. Mustafa tiptoed into the room where his mother lay with the new baby. Here and there around the room were gifts which the neighbors had brought, gifts for Zübeyde and gifts for that small red bundle Makbule. No one looked now at Mustafa. Everyone was looking at that new baby. Mustafa didn't even want to see the baby any more. He scuffed out of the room and went to one of the large bay windows overlooking the street. He peered through the shutter. From there he could see the *simit* (large pretzellike cracker) sellers balancing their *simit* trays on their heads. He could watch the water sellers trade a glassful of water for a coin. He could see the gypsy ironmongers plying their noisy trade, and the street cleaners sweeping with their knobby brooms, and the black-mantled women going off to market. Off in the distance he could even see the snow-topped slopes of Mount Olympus. There, too, he could hear the clang of the horse-drawn cars on Vardar Street and the Greek church bells and the deep-throated hooting of the ships in the harbor. And five times a day he could hear the muezzin (Moslem chanter of the call to prayer, intoned from the mosque minaret) summoning the faithful to prayer and to praise of Allah. All these sights and sounds were much more interesting to any boy than a little new baby could be.

Mustafa's greatest pleasure, especially in the wintertime, was to feed the small sweet-voiced goldfinches which flocked to their balcony. Zübeyde did not like to have Mustafa out on the balcony in the cold. He was now her only son, and he must on no account become ill. Still, Mustafa wanted to feed the birds. "See, Mother," he said. "The poor things are hungry. Look how they come to me for seeds. Don't worry. As soon as I fill these dishes with seeds, I'll come inside and watch them through the window." And so he did.

One day when Mustafa was five years old, he went with his mother to visit one of her friends. While they were walking through the busy marketplace, Mustafa asked one question after another. It seemed that he heard every sound and saw every sight and smelled every smell — the customers with round loaves of bread under their arms and vegetables strung on raffia dangling from their hands, the hawking of fruits and vegetables and cheese, the bustling of the *hamals* (porters) with great wicker baskets strapped on their backs, the clanking of the cups of the water sellers, the smell of spices spread out for sale. Then suddenly his questions stopped. Mustafa had disappeared.

Zübeyde looked everywhere for her son, first among the vegetable booths and along the clothing booths, next in the deafening din of the tinsmiths' stands, and finally just outside the open market, where men sat under big plane trees selling captive goldfinches. It was there that Zübeyde found Mustafa, bargaining with a bearded peasant for two small birds. Zübeyde stood aside, curious to see what her son would do. Mustafa shook his head firmly as the peasant stated his price. Then the peasant shook his head firmly as Mustafa named a price. Finally he agreed that Mustafa could have the two birds for two *kuruş* (a total of about eight cents), since the child refused to pay any more. He took two birds from the cage and handed them to Mustafa. The boy held them tenderly in his cupped hands. How little they were, and how frightened! He blew gently on them. Their downy feathers stirred. Their round eyes stared at him.

Zübeyde hurried up to Mustafa. "My boy, what are you going to do with those birds? We have no cage for them, and you *know* you can't take them where we are going visiting." Her face was flushed with annoyance as she waited for his answer.

"Why, Mother," he said, "I didn't buy these birds to put them in a cage. I bought them to set them free. Birds need to be free to fly, and to sing. Watch!" And the boy released one of the goldfinches. It fluffed up its feathers and then it flew free, up to a branch of the plane tree. There it perched, singing so gay a song that Zübeyde had to smile. Then he opened his cupped hands to release the

21

second bird. It, too, spread its wings and flew up into the plane tree, where it perched to sing. "There. You see, Mother? Nothing likes to be kept in a cage. They are happy now. Hear them sing!"

With one last look at the birds, Mustafa hurried along after his mother. They were already late for tea at the home of Afet Hanım (*Hanım* is a title of respect for women). As they hurried, Zübeyde thought about this son of hers. Surely he was unlike the children she had had before. He would bear watching.

That night at dinner she told Ali Riza about Mustafa's bargaining outside the marketplace. Ali Riza was pleased. "You are right, my boy," he said. "Two *kuruş* is a very small price to pay for freedom. Birds are like people. They need to be free. A cage is no better than a prison. You did well to set them free.

"And you have learned to bargain! It will not be long until you can help me in my lumber shop, now that you are able to bargain. We can always use a clever mind in business."

"But when I grow, I do not want to work in a lumber shop, Father," said Mustafa. "I do not wish to work in *any* trade. Think! Why should a man want to carry a roll of cloth down the street on his shoulder? Perhaps I shall be a soldier. Every day, I see the officers going past to the Konak (two-story brick government office building on Sabri Paşa Caddesi, a main thoroughfare) with their fine uniforms and their great curved swords. Yes, perhaps I shall be a soldier."

His mother shook her head, but his father smiled. "There is more to being a soldier than wearing a uniform and clanking a sword, my son," he said. "But we shall see. Meantime, you will go to school to learn to read and write. Someday, Allah willing, you will find the work which is right for you."

And then he spoke of something else, of the revolt in

Arabia against the Ottoman Sultan. "They do not like us," he sighed. "Some day we shall have serious problems with our Empire. There is unrest everywhere, especially here in Macedonia. No matter how many spies the Sultan has, he cannot discover all those who wish to do him harm. I fear for our Empire. Though we have given the foreign nations special privileges, they are not grateful. There will be a day of reckoning, and on that day, my son, many men will serve for reasons other than the uniform."

Mustafa listened as his father talked. Yes, there was truly much to learn about this world into which he had been born.

From the time he was very small, Mustafa watched other children playing in the street and by the public fountain. He had friends, among them Nuri Conker, and *they* played. But he just watched — he never played. He stood there, his hands clasped behind his back, his eyes not missing a single motion. Children would race by, playing tag. Others would play hopscotch or ball-bouncing games or a game like marbles played with sheep's knucklebones. Still, Mustafa just watched.

One day the boys were playing leapfrog, and they teased Mustafa to join them. He smiled, his head held proudly. "Of course, I shall play. But can you leap over me while I am standing upright? For I will not bend for you at all."

The boys stared at him in surprise. Then they nudged each other and laughed. This Mustafa was a strange sort of boy. And the game went on without him.

2

EARLY YEARS AT SCHOOL

WHEN Mustafa became seven years old, it was time for Ali Riza to decide which school the boy would attend. This child was bright for his age, and his education was an important matter.

In those days there were two types of schools in the Turkish quarter of Salonica. The *mahalle* ("subdistrict") school, the traditional school, was taught by either a *hafız* (one who had memorized the Koran, the Moslem holy book) or a *hoca.* In this kind of school the child was taught to read and write the Arabic script. In addition, he learned geography, a bit of history (chiefly the names of the sultans of the Ottoman Empire), and arithmetic. But most of each class day was spent in memorizing the Koran in Arabic, a language none of the students understood; for devout Moslems, the better educated a child became, the more of the Koran he could recite without error. The *mahalle* school in Ali Riza's quarter of Salonica was taught by Hafız Mehmet, known to be harsh and rough with his students, a hard teacher. Such teachers were considered the best kind for children who really wanted to learn. Parents and teachers alike professed the truth of the proverb "Roses grow where a teacher hits." Punishment and education belonged together, they thought. For this reason, Hafız Mehmet was well known and highly respected.

But there was another, newer type of school in Salonica, the kind that Ali Riza had come to admire because of its educational philosophy. This school was taught by Şemsi Efendi. Unlike the *hafız* teachers, Şemsi Efendi had not been satisfied with the old method of teaching. He had done much studying and reading of his own, and he believed that learning came best when students were really interested in getting answers for their own questions. He hoped to teach in such a way that learning would become a pleasure rather than a burden. It was this school, founded in 1878, to which Ali Riza wished to send Mustafa.

But Zübeyde wanted Mustafa to go to the traditional kind of school, the school where the Koran was taught and where boys could get the good, old-fashioned, respectable kind of education they needed for living in the Ottoman Empire. Such a beginning would bring her boy good luck and many blessings, she believed.

There was a special ceremony held for boys who entered the *mahalle* school. The parents served *şerbet* (a fruit drink) and *baklava* (a honeyed pastry) to the many guests who came. Hafız Mehmet himself led a procession of his pupils to the new student's home, where they feasted on sweets with the family and friends. Then the new pupil walked at the head of the procession with the teacher, with all of them singing hymns and chanting amens. All the boys were dressed in their best clothing, and everyone admired the fine procession. This was the kind of special treatment Zübeyde wanted for her bright, handsome son, her Mustafa.

Mustafa kept silent while his parents quarreled this way and that about his school. He was shy of ceremonies and wished only to be started at this business of learning. He was embarrassed to be taken to school in a grand procession, with singing so that all could hear. Little by little, the answer to the problem became clear: Because his mother wished it, he would be enrolled in Hafız Mehmet's school. Then soon afterwards, he would be moved to Şemsi Efendi's school, where he could get the kind of education that Ali Riza felt would best fit him for the fast-changing world in which he lived.

All this argument had already taken a month of valuable school time. Ali Riza went at once to Hafız Mehmet and told him of their decision to enroll Mustafa. The following week, the gaily dressed procession came to Mustafa's house for the traditional feasting. Zübeyde watched proudly as the sweet *şerbet* was passed again and again, and as the guests devoured the delicious *baklava*. Ali Riza, knowing how his shy son felt about such ceremony, took him aside and gave him a handsome schoolbag, decorated with gold sequins, and with a fine alphabet book inside. On top of the schoolbag was a *maşallah* (a good-luck emblem meaning "May Allah bless him") to bring him good fortune. But Mustafa was not comforted. "How I wish you could just *take* me to school, Father," he muttered. His face was tense and unhappy.

'Be patient, my son, for just a month or so. Learn at Hafız Mehmet's school to read and write your Arabic alphabet. Then I shall take you myself to Şemsi Efendi's school. We must satisfy your mother first. Then, my son, we shall satisfy ourselves!"

So Mustafa was patient. He walked to the school at

26

the head of the procession, carrying his new schoolbag, which after all was very handsome. His father murmured to Mustafa's teacher the traditional expression "His flesh is yours and his bones are mine." (This means that the parent would respect whatever methods the teacher used to enforce learning, especially physical punishment.) And then Mustafa began to learn his alphabet.

Day after day the boys knelt and recited in unison the endless letters of the Arabic alphabet. After they had practiced their letters, they recited in unison various prayers from the Koran, all in Arabic, a language still meaningless to them. Day after day some boy or another was beaten for his disobedience or his inattention. Finally one day Mustafa tired of kneeling to learn. "They don't kneel to learn at Şemsi Efendi's school," he said defiantly. "I shall not kneel to learn. I shall *sit*, instead." And indeed he sat.

While Hafız Mehmet pondered what to do with this insolent boy, the rest cried, "We too shall sit to learn." And *they* sat. For this kind of rebellion Hafız Mehmet had no answer. And as long as Mustafa continued in that school, the boys sat to memorize their letters and their prayers.

Night after night, Mustafa recited his letters to his father, and wrote them painstakingly in his copybook. At last he had mastered the whole alphabet. It was time now to start his schooling with Şemsi Efendi. The very next day, Ali Riza himself took Mustafa to Şemsi Efendi's school. From then on, learning became pleasant to Mustafa.

Now that Mustafa was attending a school where questions were encouraged, he found he had questions by the thousands to ask. He asked questions at school, and he asked questions at home, questions about things he was learning at school, about things he overheard on the streets and in the shops, about things that every boy wonders about. Ali Riza was delighted to see how eager his son was to learn, and of course he wondered what kind of work Mustafa was doing at school. He went therefore to ask Şemsi Efendi how Mustafa behaved himself and what kind of student he was.

"Mustafa is a remarkable boy," answered Şemsi Efendi. "He is alert, quick to grasp what is said, very eager to learn things, and entirely attentive. It is easy to tell that Mustafa is a clever boy by the questions that he asks. Does he also ask questions at home?"

"Ask questions? He most certainly does," said Ali Riza.

"Mustafa is going to make a better student than you can even imagine," continued Şemsi Efendi. "He is brighter than any of the other students in his class, so there should be no question in your mind about him. Above all else, you must avoid urging him to study. He will pursue learning more eagerly if you leave him alone."

True enough, Mustafa finished his first year at Şemsi Efendi's school with the highest marks of all. He especially enjoyed arithmetic, and spent much time at home constructing problems and working out the answers for himself. His father, who enjoyed learning too, took great pleasure in Mustafa's interest and his success.

Mustafa was interested not only in schoolwork, but in everything he saw going on around him. One day a carpenter came to repair a bedroom door at their house. As usual, Mustafa stood there watching the carpenter.

"Mustafa, come here!" his mother called.

"Please let me watch a little while!" Mustafa called back, and he continued to watch. Suddenly from where he was standing, he saw the door slip from its hinge at the top. "Hasan Usta!" (*usta* is a title of respect for a workman or employe) he said excitedly. "Let me help you."

"Just stand aside, my boy," the carpenter said gruffly, intent on what he was doing.

At that moment, the door slipped entirely free from its hinges and fell on Hasan Usta, tumbling him from the chair on which he had been standing. The carpenter got up again, but his hand had been cut and was bleeding.

"Mother, Mother!" called Mustafa, and he ran to his mother to get help for the carpenter. But when he came to his mother, he found that she had fainted. Mustafa stood there, frightened, not knowing what to do.

In a moment or two, Zübeyde stirred, and then she opened her eyes, to find Mustafa looking down at her. She sat up. "Mustafa, are you all right?" she asked anxiously.

"Of course, Mother. But Hasan Usta cut his hand and it's bleeding. Can you come?"

"In a minute, Mustafa, in a minute. But how you frightened me! I called you, and when you didn't come I was afraid for you. Once when you were just a baby and your father was away from home, burglars entered our house at night by taking a door off its hinges. They leaned the door against the wall of the room where you were sleeping, while they searched the house for whatever they could find. I heard a noise, and came with a candle to see what was wrong. The burglars scooped up whatever they could find and ran out, tripping over the door as they went. The door fell across your bed, and I was afraid you had been killed. But when the maid and I lifted the door from the bed, there you lay, sound asleep. The door had hit the sides of the bed and a chair which was at the foot of the bed. Imagine! You were perfectly safe, after all! Still, I worry about you every time I hear something fall."

"Look, Mother." Mustafa laughed and held out his

29

arms. "I am all right this time, too. But Hasan Usta is not. Come and see his hand." And Mustafa and his mother went to attend to Hasan Usta's cut.

Those days were exciting ones for Mustafa. But matters were not going well for Ali Riza, his father. His lumber shop had proved to be unprofitable, his investment in the salt business had brought heavy losses, and he was constantly worried about providing adequately for his family. Soon there would be another child, and how could he support another child? Discouragement began to affect his health. At last he became quite ill (of intestinal tuberculosis, and — some suggest — of a liver ailment), and he was unable to go to work. For many long months he suffered.

Day after day, Mustafa hurried home from school to tell his father how the day had gone. Every day his father smiled to see Mustafa's happiness. He did not want Mustafa to know how ill he was, and his illness was never discussed in the family. The maid took Mustafa to school every day, since his father was unable to take him, and she came to call for him in the afternoon. For Mustafa, life went on almost as usual.

But one afternoon he came home from school to find his Uncle Hüseyin, Zübeyde's brother, in the living room. His uncle's face was white and serious. Mustafa knew at once that something was terribly wrong. He ran to his father's room and found his mother there, crying. Greatly upset, he tried to comfort his mother by saying, "Don't cry, Mother. Who can stop a sick man from dying? Look! You still have me, your son Mustafa." Then, realizing suddenly what his father's death would mean to him, he sat down on the steps and sobbed for his father, the one who most of all had loved and understood him.

3

LEARNING TO LIVE ON
THE FARM AT RAPLA

A daughter, Naciye, had been born to Zübeyde just forty days before Ali Riza's death. Since the sale of the lumber business had brought very little, Zübeyde knew that she could no longer afford to live in Salonica with her children. As soon as Naciye was old enough to live safely in the country, Zübeyde and her children must rent out their house in Salonica and go to live with her brother Hüseyin. Hüseyin, a bachelor, supervised the farm belonging to Süleyman (some say Abdürrahman) at Rapla, twenty miles or so from Salonica. Until they moved to Rapla, Mustafa would continue to attend Şemsi Efendi's school.

So that Mustafa could finish his primary schooling, Zübeyde and her children stayed in Salonica longer than they could comfortably manage. But when he had graduated from Şemsi Efendi's school (in 1891, at the age of ten), Zübeyde decided that the rest of the family must now be considered. She found someone to rent her home, and she and her children went to Rapla.

This was the beginning of a whole new life for Mustafa and his sisters. For ten years, Mustafa had rubbed shoulders with all kinds of people, rich and poor, and had grown accustomed to the opportunities and sights and sounds of city life. Now suddenly he found himself in the open country, with green fields stretching as far as he could see on all sides of the farmhouse, with sunshine and fresh air and animals of all kinds, and useful work that a boy could do.

Morning on the farm at Rapla began early, with Zübeyde waking the children by sprinkling water in their faces. Mustafa, eager for the day's activities, dressed quickly and ran downstairs and outside to the spring, a hundred meters or so from the house. The pleasure of splashing himself in the cold spring water was only one of the delights he found in his new life. Even the food tasted fresher, and seemed more bountiful, with all the milk and butter and cheese a boy could want. On winter mornings, cold milk gave way to *salep* (milk with sugar and a thickening agent called *salep* in it), a warm drink for a good start on a cold day. Winter evenings, too, brought a special treat: each of the children had three chestnuts to roast in the fire. And, best of all, Zübeyde's mother, Ayşe, was at hand, enjoying the children and answering their questions and telling them stories.

Mustafa plunged so eagerly into this new life on the farm that his mother became alarmed. "Look at him!" she exclaimed one day to Hüseyin. "He has become a regular peasant!"

Her brother laughed. "Leave the boy alone, Zübeyde. This is only another kind of learning. He needs to walk barefooted in the mud and help with the planting

32

and harvesting and learn how farmers live. He will grow strong and healthy, and be a better man for it."

Still, Zübeyde was disturbed about her son's further education. They tried one means after another to find a suitable teacher for Mustafa in the country. Finally they had tried everything but the Greek Orthodox school, taught by a priest. People in the area thought highly of this priest, and Zübeyde decided to send Mustafa there to school. Uncle Hüseyin took him there the first day on horseback. For the whole day, Mustafa sat in the schoolroom with children who smiled behind his back — or so he thought — at his strange speech. He listened to the teacher speaking in Greek, a language he did not understand, about things that all the other children seemed to know. He wanted above all else to learn, but here in this school there was no door to knowledge for him. The whole day long he sat, in a babble of tongues, facing a crucifix bearing the figure of Christ. All his old feelings about Hafız Mehmet's school rushed back upon him. How could he learn in such a place?

At last his uncle came to take him home. "Well, Mustafa, did you like the school?" he asked as he helped the boy to mount.

Mustafa did not answer in words, but his face was long and unhappy. They rode in silence for awhile toward Rapla. Finally Mustafa began to ask questions about places they passed, and about birds that they saw in flight. Still, he said nothing of the school. Uncle Hüseyin knew Mustafa well enough to understand his feelings, and asked him no more questions about the day at school.

That evening at dinner, Zübeyde asked, "Mustafa, do you want to go back to the Greek school tomorrow?"

"No, Mother," he said. "I'll not go back to the church."

"Why do you call it a church, Son? It's a school."

"Perhaps, Mother, but it is far too much like Hafız Mehmet's school. I did not understand Hafız Mehmet's language and I do not understand the priest's language."

"Be patient, my son. You will understand the priest's language in a few weeks."

"I am sorry, Mother," said Mustafa, "but I cannot go to a church school, whether it be Moslem or Greek. I cannot learn in such a place."

No more was said of the school that evening, and Mustafa never returned to it. He read the books that he found at the farmhouse, and he spent many hours thinking of what he might be when he was grown. Still, he came no nearer an answer to this most important question.

Uncle Hüseyin, in an effort to interest the boy, one day brought him a pistol from Salonica. "Here, my boy," he said. "You are old enough now to learn to shoot."

Mustafa examined the gun eagerly. "How do you load it, Uncle Hüseyin?" he asked. And patiently his uncle explained how the gun was cleaned, and loaded, and fired. After dinner that evening they went out into the field, and Mustafa learned to shoot the pistol.

After Mustafa had gone to bed that night, Zübeyde talked with Hüseyin about the gun. "I wish you had waited until he was a little older, my brother. A ten-year-old boy is too young to handle a gun. Suppose he should have an accident?" And she shuddered at the thought.

"Mustafa is a very keen child, Zübeyde. Don't worry. I was beside him all the time he was shooting. He has learned to take good aim. A man should learn to use a gun well. I shall never leave the child alone while he is shooting."

After Mustafa had learned to shoot, he went out with his uncle late every afternoon to practice. Following his practice, it was his responsibility to clean the gun and leave it ready for use the next time. One evening as usual he went to his room to clean his gun, and as usual Makbule offered to help him. It was her job to hand him the rags and the oil and the brush as he needed them. She had just laid out what he needed and had stepped back a little distance to watch him work when suddenly the gun went off, and the room was filled with smoke. Makbule could not see her brother, and she began to cry, "My brother is dead! My brother is dead!"

As the smoke cleared, they saw their mother in the doorway, with her face as white as paper and her eyes fixed directly on Mustafa. "See what you have done! You have shot your sister!"

"No, Mother, I am all right," said Makbule. And for a wonder, no harm had been done at all. But Mustafa never again cleaned a gun without removing all the bullets.

Uncle Hüseyin loved to hunt, and Mustafa was eager to learn to hunt, too. Seeing the boy's desire to learn, Hüseyin taught him how to load and unload a rifle. Then he showed the boy how to aim, and they spent long hours in practice.

At this time, Mustafa was taking care of a flock of pigeons, and he was concerned about the hawks that flew above the farm and now and then pounced on one of his pigeons. One day as a hawk circled above the pigeons, Mustafa ran to the house for his uncle's rifle. This time, no pigeon would be caught! He took careful aim and fired. The first time, he missed. The second time, the hawk came circling to the ground.

"Good work, Mustafa!" called his uncle, who had come just in time to see the second shot. "But stay where you are. Don't move at all."

Mustafa obeyed his uncle, and waited to see what his uncle had to say about the hawk. "You aimed well, my boy. That was a fine shot. I warned you to wait because it is dangerous to try to pick up a hawk you have shot. Hawks are utterly fearless. If they are not dead, they bite you terribly when you try to touch them." They walked then to find the fierce bird. It was lying beside a bush, and there were already ants crawling between its feathers. Mustafa had killed it with that one shot.

"Well, my boy," said Uncle Hüseyin, "I think the time has come to take you hunting with me. Do you have good walking legs? Hunting takes a great deal of walking, you know."

"Just try me once," said Mustafa earnestly. "I'll walk as long as you will. When shall we go, Uncle Hüseyin?"

"We'll go on Saturday." And Mustafa began to count the days.

At last Saturday came. Mustafa was up well before dawn, and dressed to go. His mother came into the kitchen as they were eating a hurried breakfast. "Do be careful, Hüseyin," she begged. "Remember, he is just a boy."

Hüseyin and Mustafa looked quickly at each other. Each had the same thought. Wasn't it like a mother to be worried!

It was toward supper time when they returned. When they came in, Zübeyde exclaimed, "Mustafa, you are covered with dust. What a pity! What did you bring? Where is your bag?"

"Of course, Mother, a hunter gets dusty because he lies on the ground to take aim, and because he walks and walks. Osman Çavuş (*çavuş* means "sergeant") has my bag. Uncle Hüseyin gave it to him to carry so I would not become tired while I was walking. When Osman brings my bag, you will see what is in it. I brought down a bird with every shot. Now I'll go and wash." He stumbled wearily as he went to wash and change his clothes, but he never said a word about being tired.

Mustafa had come back to the kitchen by the time

36

Osman Çavuş came in with his bag. Eagerly his mother opened the bag and took out — six dead crows! When Zübeyde saw them, she could not help laughing. "Son, couldn't you find something better to shoot? Crows are no good for eating! And why take the trouble to carry them all the way home?"

"But, Mother," said Mustafa, "whenever you see a crow, you talk about how harmful they are. They eat the seeds when we sow them; they steal the nuts we pick from the trees, and they fly away with your soap if you leave it outside. Now there are six crows less. Isn't that worth talking about?"

All the same, after he had shot the crows, Mustafa was sad about them. Perhaps those were not the crows which had eaten the seeds, or stolen the nuts, or swooped to pick up the soap that had been left outside . . . Somehow, he was no longer quite so eager to go hunting again. Perhaps he would hunt only to protect his pigeons. Hawks were clearly more harmful than crows. And so it was that Mustafa and Uncle Hüseyin spoke no more of hunting.

With this new life in the country, Mustafa grew strong and healthy. He was up early in the morning, washing in the small stream that passed the farmhouse. He spent long hours in the horsebean (broad-bean) fields with his sister Makbule, scaring away the crows from the crop. It was during such times that he and Makbule learned to know each other well and to enjoy each other's company.

There was a small hut in the middle of the horsebean field in which the children could sit to watch for crows. When crows appeared, they would run out and wave their arms wildly to frighten the crows and drive them away. As the crows became accustomed to the children, they were less easily frightened. One afternoon a large flock of crows came together and descended upon the hut. The weight and the motion were sufficient to tumble the roof in upon the two children, who had been trying to drive them away with sticks. Makbule was half buried by the straw roof, and she began to cry. Mustafa became very angry and, taking off his jacket, he tied it to a long stick. He waved this stick feverishly at the crows with one hand and pulled away the straw from his sister with the other. That night at dinner they had an exciting tale indeed to tell their mother and Uncle Hüseyin.

Mustafa was always making one thing or another from bits and pieces of materials that he found around the farm. One day he came to Makbule with a board.

"Here. Hold this," he said.

"What for?" she asked.

"Never mind. Just *hold* it." And he cut and hammered, and before long he had made a sort of musical instrument, a *tambur* (Oriental guitar), all except for the strings. When his uncle saw it, he sent to Salonica for strings to make it usable, and in a little while Mustafa was able to coax a tune from it as he had heard the hired man Osman Çavuş do.

"Play us a folksong, Mustafa," his uncle urged.

Mustafa straightened up to his full height. "My uncle," he said firmly, "I didn't make this *tambur* to play folksongs. I made it so I could play the 'March of Osman Paşa' (*paşa*, or *pasha*, is the title for a high-ranking official, especially a military officer — a general) to which my father marched when he was a first lieutenant in the war against Serbia." And he practiced patiently until he could play the March.

One day Mustafa set to work on something in the front yard of the house in which his mother and her children lived, close to Uncle Hüseyin's house. He was sawing and hammering, sawing and hammering. This time, he refused to let Makbule see what he was making. Finally he took her with him to the spring which flowed into the stream running past the house. He had made a little dam, and a little farther away there was something like a box, with a propeller turning.

"What is it?" she asked.

"It is a water mill," he answered.

"Show me the grinding stones, then."

"This will soon be a flour mill, Makbush (his nickname for Makbule). It has no grinding stones yet, but just watch the propeller turn! Isn't it wonderful?" And the two played with the water mill until the hired man came to tell them that their mother was calling them for dinner.

But what pleased Makbule most was the little hut her brother built not far from the farmhouse. He had finished it after many days of hard work. The hut looked rather like a tent. The top and the sides were covered with straw matting. There were two steps leading to the open door. It had seats in it, and shelves to put things on. In front of the hut they made a garden, where they very carefully planted some flowers. Often their mother and grandmother came to visit them in their hut, and this pleased the children immensely.

One day Uncle Hüseyin came to the hut shortly before lunch time for a visit. "Why, where is Mustafa?" he asked.

"He went to get some water, Uncle Hüseyin. We want to water the flowers," Makbule answered.

"Fine. Let me sit here and watch you. I want to see how you two young farmers water your garden."

While Uncle Hüseyin was speaking, Mustafa came with a pail of water in each hand. "Be ready to sprinkle them, Makbush. Quickly!"

Then he saw his uncle. "Welcome to our hut, Uncle Hüseyin," he said proudly. "Won't you go inside?"

Uncle Hüseyin answered, "I am very comfortable on the steps. I see you are carrying some water."

"Yes, Uncle Hüseyin. We are going to water our flowers. I carry the pails, and Makbule sprinkles the water on the flowers. But we can do that later, just before we eat our lunch."

"Oh, but you can't, my boy," Uncle Hüseyin said, shaking his head.

"*Why* can't we water our flowers then?" asked Makbule curiously.

"Because you would be watering them when the sun is high in the sky," Uncle Hüseyin answered. "You must water flowers during the cool of the day."

"That's strange, Uncle," Mustafa said. "I was thinking when we were thirsty the flowers were thirsty. I'm always thirstiest when the sun is hot. I water my flowers then to make them cool."

His uncle smiled and shook his head. "If you water plants in the hot sun, the drops evaporate and cause the leaves to burn. By the way, what kind of fertilizer did you use on your plants?"

"Fertilizer?" Mustafa was puzzled.

"Yes, my boy. It's a kind of food for plants. It is not only people who get hungry. Plants get hungry, too, for things they can't get from the earth. They have no tongues and cannot say they are hungry, but a good farmer knows when his plants are hungry. He can tell by the looks of the leaves and the stalks."

"And are our plants hungry, Uncle?" asked Makbule.

'Yes, they are, Makbule. But you must not give them too *much* food, either. Too much food makes plants ill, just as it does people."

Mustafa sighed. "Uncle Hüseyin, there is a great deal for farmers to know!"

"You are right, Mustafa. Being a good farmer is not easy," said his uncle. "You must love the earth. For those who love the earth, the earth becomes fertile.

40

Now come with me and get some fertilizer. Later you will see how well your flowers grow." And in a little while, true enough, their garden began to look much better.

Soon the warm summer days were over. The weather became cold, and the rains began. Day after day the children stayed in the farmhouse, wondering all the while what was happening to their hut. Finally one day the rain stopped, and a weak and rather watery-looking sun shone. "There is no use to ask Mother. It's muddy outdoors, and she'd surely say 'no,'" said Mustafa. "But I'm going out anyway to look at our hut. Promise not to tell!"

"I promise," said Makbule, wishing she could go, too. And Mustafa went quietly down the stairs and out the door.

Makbule watched him as long as he was in sight, and then she began to play with her dolls. After a long while, she heard a strange swishing noise at her window. She ran to the window to look, and there she saw a broom at the end of a stick. Holding the other end of the stick was Mustafa. He was shivering with the cold, and he asked Makbule to throw down to him a piece of burlap so that he could wipe his muddy bare feet before he came into the house.

Makbule found the piece of burlap, but she was too small to lift the heavy window. While she was still trying to open it, her mother heard the noise and came into the room. "What are you doing? And *where* is Mustafa?" she asked.

Of course, Makbule didn't answer. Hadn't she promised not to tell? But her mother came to the window and saw Mustafa all muddy and cold. "Mustafa! Come in at once!" she called.

Mustafa didn't want to come in just then. He knew his mother was cross. But he had no other choice.

41

"Where are your shoes?" she asked, shocked to find him barefooted in the mud.

"I took them off before I went to the hut. They're on the porch, and they aren't a bit muddy," he said proudly.

"You went to the hut? *Barefooted?*" Zübeyde was almost speechless, she was so astonished. Of course, Mustafa was roundly scolded, and dressed warmly to ward off a cold. And for weeks after that time, the children didn't have a chance to go outside.

4

THE STORY OF ALI RIZA
AND THE BANDITS

THOSE LONG, WET WINTER DAYS, Mustafa and Makbule
played inside. In the evenings they roasted chestnuts in
the glowing fire. And, what was best, they listened to
their grandmother as she told them stories.

"Tell me about our father," said Mustafa one night.
"Did anything exciting ever happen to him?"

"Yes, indeed," his grandmother answered. "But
perhaps it is too frightening a story to be told before
bedtime." She looked at Zübeyde. "I'm thinking of the
bandits," she said. "Do you wish . . .?" Zübeyde shook her
head. That was much too worrisome a story to tell to
children.

But the children had caught the word "bandits," and
they were determined to hear the story.

"Bandits, bandits," little Makbule chanted.

And, "Oh, please, Grandmother, tell us the story!" begged Mustafa. And the grandmother, who liked nothing better than to please these bright-eyed children, settled herself comfortably on the cushioned bench and began to talk.

"It happened before you were born, Mustafa — when Ahmet and Ömer were very little boys. Your mother and your father were living in Cayağızı, on the slopes of Mount Olympus, where he was a government official in the Customs Administration. That was a bad time to live in Cayagızı, because there were bandits who lived in the mountains there. Often they would kidnap people and hold them for ransom.

"Those bandits were very bold and dangerous men, and no one was safe from them. One day several bandits came close to your father's house. Your mother was in the big garden walking with Ahmet, and Ömer was sleeping nearby in his cradle. The bandits stood there watching your mother, who was a very beautiful woman. Should they kidnap her and take her to the mountains? Or should they kidnap her husband, Ali Riza? He would surely pay a big ransom for his life. They watched a while longer, and then they crept away quietly to lay their plans.

"A few days later, Ali Riza got an unsigned letter written by one of those bandits. It said, 'I came a few days ago to kidnap your wife. You have a very beautiful wife. She is worth a large ransom. Several times your son came so near to me that I almost reached out to pet him. I have a son that age at home, myself. I know you are a good man. You never give trouble to others. I saw how happy your son was to see you. I wanted to kidnap all of you for ransom. Instead, I am asking you to pay me something. I want ten gold watches. You cannot find good watches here. You must bring them from Salonica. I will give you one week to bring them here. I will tell you later what you

44

must do with the watches.'

"Your father's voice shook as he read the letter to your mother. 'For many months I have been afraid of this,' he said. 'I did not want to tell you about the bandits because I did not want to worry you. But you and the children must return at once to Salonica. It is far too dangerous to stay here any longer. I have spoken to Captain Vasilaki about taking you in his small ship to Salonica. Pack your things tonight. Early tomorrow morning, before the sun rises, you and the children must be aboard that ship.'

"'I will not go,' said your mother. 'If you must stay here, then I shall stay here, too.'

"But your father was determined. 'You will not be alone on the ship,' he said. 'There will be another Turkish woman aboard. But you must be very careful not to tell that woman about the letter I received from the bandits. I have written a letter to my mother about the watches. She will give them to Captain Vasilaki, but don't tell him what is in the packet. Go, now, and pack your things.'

"The next morning when the ship set out for Salonica, your mother and Ahmet and Ömer were aboard. The captain had given your mother his own cabin. As soon as your mother had stopped crying, she went out on deck to talk with the other Turkish woman. Her son and his wife and two children had been kidnapped by bandits near Cayağızı and a very large ransom had been asked for them. The woman sold her house and her fields and everything else that she had in order to raise the money for the ransom. But when she got to Cayağızı with the ransom money, she was given terrible news. The bandits had been angry because she had not given them the money right away. They had killed her son and his family."

The children shuddered. Zübeyde shook her head

again. "Please, Mother. This is too much for the children."

But Mustafa had not heard enough. "What happened to my father?" he demanded. "You said something exciting happened to my father with the bandits. Please tell us, Grandmother."

With a little shrug of her shoulders, their grandmother went on telling the story. "After your mother left Cayağızı with the two boys, she went on to live with your father's mother and sister in their home near Salonica. It was in that house that your sister Fatma had been born."

"Fatma!" exclaimed Makbule. "When did we have a sister Fatma?"

Zübeyde began to cry, and the grandmother shook her head at Makbule. "There is a story about Fatma, a sad story, and it must wait for another time. I was telling you about your father and the bandits."

"Yes, yes, Grandmother," said Mustafa. "That is the story we want to hear."

"Well, then," said his grandmother, "your mother and the others in that house waited every day for the news from Cayağızı. Captain Vasilaki came to Salonica regularly with loads of charcoal from Cayağızı, and each time he came, your Uncle Hüseyin met him at the wharf in the harbor to ask for news of Ali Riza. For weeks, the news was good. Then suddenly Captain Vasilaki brought no news at all. Hüseyin thought that the Captain knew some bad news about Ali Riza that he was unwilling to tell, so your uncle asked several other captains in the harbor. At last one captain said, 'Yes, it is true. Ali Riza has been carried away by bandits. They have already held him captive for a week, and all in Cayağızı fear for his safety. The bandits do not usually keep their captives long, you know. Please forgive me. This is very bad news for his family."

46

"When your uncle came to the house that day, he was very pale and silent. He did not need to tell them the news. They could see in his face that something dreadful had happened to Ali Riza.

"For many weeks, no further news came about Ali Riza. Hüseyin came one evening and begged your mother to take the children and go to live with me, her mother. 'Zübeyde,' he said, 'you know as well as I that the bandits never keep a prisoner alive this long. Ali Riza must surely be dead. How can you be away from your own family at such a time as this?'

"Your mother stared at him sadly. 'My brother, I must stay here,' she said. 'Surely word will come soon. And Ali Riza's mother loves Ahmet and Ömer dearly. How could she bear to part with them when her heart is already breaking over her lost son?' So your mother stayed on in that house.

"That very night there was a loud ringing of the bell at the front door. Your mother awoke with fear in her heart. 'Please Allah, may it not be bad news!' she whispered. The bell rang again, and she hurried toward the door. But Ali Riza's mother had run there before her.

"'Who is it?' she called through the door.

"'It is Ali,' a voice said.

"'Ali!' exclaimed your mother, and she shook with excitement.

"'It cannot be Ali. That is not his voice,' your grandmother said.

"A voice came through the door again. 'Open the door, Mother. I am Ali.'

"'Ali died a long while ago,' said his mother. 'I won't open the door to a stranger.'

"Again the voice came. 'Open, Mother. Don't be afraid. I am ill and exhausted. Please don't make me wait here.'

"She opened the door, and it really was Ali Riza. He

walked slowly. His clothes were torn, his hair uncombed. His mother and Zübeyde looked at him, unable to say a word. "Well, how are Ahmet and Ömer?" Ali Riza asked. But his mother and Zübeyde scarcely heard the question, they were crying so for joy and relief.

"Your father badly needed rest, and he had not eaten anything for two days. By this time, the whole household was awake, and everyone was rejoicing to see him. All he wanted to do was sleep, so he went upstairs to bed.

"As soon as he was able, he told all of us what had happened. He had given the gold watches to the bandits as soon as Captain Vasilaki had brought them. For a little while, he was safe. Then one night he received a message that the chief of the bandits was coming to meet him on a certain corner. He took his gun and went to the meeting place near the harbor, but no one was there. Suddenly bandits came from everywhere, and he was surrounded. They took his money and his gun and his watch. One of the men spoke to him, and he recognized that the voice belonged to the bandit to whom he had given the watches. 'Goodbye,' said this man. 'I will see you in the other world.' The bandits left two of their men to guard your father while they gathered together to decide what to do with him.

"While the guards were with Ali Riza, one of them said to him, 'They should give the decision quickly. There are six other victims waiting for decisions. You are a rich man, Ali Riza. If our captain questions you, keep nothing secret. The captain's name is Orestes. Whatever Orestes says, obey him.'

"Suddenly someone called, 'Bring that man here.'

"The guard said, 'Walk on. The captain wants you.'

"Captain Orestes seemed a young man, tall and bearded. He asked, 'Are you Ali Riza from Salonica?'

"'Yes,' your father answered.

House in Salonica identified by the following plaque: "The great Turkish hero, Atatürk, was born in this house."

Waterfront at Salonica, rebuilt after a disastrous fire in 1917. Behind the famous White Tower (seen well left of center) lies the old portion of Salonica in which Atatürk was born. Photograph © National Geographic Society, included by permission of the National Geographic Society.

Photograph of Atatürk's father, Ali Riza Bey (reproduced from an original hanging on the wall in the Salonica residence).

Photograph of Atatürk's mother, Zübeyde Hanım (reproduced from one of two extant hand-colored pr furnished by Müdür Ziya Onaran, of the Türk Inkıl Müsesi in Ankara).

A street in Ankara (Angora) in the mid-1920s at the time that ancient site was chosen as the capital of the Turkish Republic. Photograph reproduced from *A Turkish Kaleidoscope*, by Clare Sheridan (New York: Dodd, Mead & Company, 1926), by courtesy of the publisher.

A market scene in Ankara (Angora) in the mid-1920s. Photograph reproduced from *A Turkish Kaleidoscope*, by Clare Sheridan (New York: Dodd, Mead & Company, 1926), by courtesy of the publisher.

This method of plowing, shown as still used in parts of Turkey, was also used in Macedonia and, without question, on the farm at Rapla while Mustafa lived there. Photograph © National Geographic Society, included by permission of the National Geographic Society. Both this photograph and the Salonica waterfront scene appeared initially in color as illustrations for the article "From Athens to Istanbul," by Jean and Franc Shor, published in the January 1956 *National Geographic*.

Women beating *bulgur* (cooked wheat) to remove the hulls, a farm task at Rapla in the late nineteenth century, during Mustafa Kemal's residence there, just as it is today in rural Turkey. Photograph provided by Ahmet E. Uysal and used with permission.

Harvesting at Çardak village, Nevsehir, Turkey, in the 1970s in the same fashion as that used on the farm at Rapla during the time Mustafa Kemal lived there. Photograph provided by Ahmet E. Uysal and used with permission.

Photograph of Mustafa Kemal's influential
elementary-school teacher, Şemsi Efendi.

Mustafa Kemal as a
graduate of the War
Academy (1902).

"'Perhaps we will decide tomorrow,' the captain said. 'Tonight you think: How much money can you give to save yourself from death? We have no knowledge of the business of customs officials.'

"As the guards walked along with Ali Riza, they were talking about the other victims. One must pay 500 gold liras, another 150 liras. That one they had been feeding for a whole month and he had still not paid. He was to be killed, they said.

"Suddenly the two guards stopped and told Ali Riza to sit down. He sat down, and he was so tired that he fell sound asleep. He awakened at a terrible shriek. One of the victims had been beheaded."

The grandmother stopped. "Are you sure you want to hear the rest? It is not a pretty story."

Makbule was nodding sleepily in the corner and she did not answer, but Mustafa said, "Oh, please, Grandmother, finish the story. I want to know how my father escaped alive from the bandits."

"Well, then," said his grandmother, "after that, they walked on a long, long way, to a road that Ali Riza had never seen before. Every day they took him walking, from one road to another. They sometimes untied his hands so that he could eat, but he was afraid to try to run away because he did not know the region well enough to find his way home. Finally the bandits decided to kill him, since they were planning another kidnapping and he was in their way.

"'We need wood for a fire,' Captain Orestes said. 'Untie Ali Riza's hands and take him with you to cut wood.'

"Ali Riza and his guards began to scramble up the hillside to reach the trees. High, high above, there was a large bare rock, and near it were some dead trees. 'It is very high,' said one guard. 'Who will go up to cut the trees?'

"'Let me go up,' Ali Riza said. 'Give me the axe and I'll cut the trees and throw the wood down to you.'

"Ali Riza cut several trees and threw down the wood. 'This is exactly the kind of wood the captain wants. Cut some more,' called one of the guards.

"Ali Riza stood for a moment looking as far as he could see. There in the distance he could see the shoreline. Now he knew where he was. He turned and began to cut down another tree. Suddenly he cried, 'Oh, I have cut myself with the axe!' He groaned and groaned. Then he sent a huge boulder rolling and crashing down the hillside. They called to him again and again, but he did not answer. He was scrambling down through the trees toward the seashore. He could hear them calling, and see them climbing up toward that high rock to search for him. Then he heard Captain Orestes say, 'He has probably fallen and killed himself. Do not say a word about this, or we will never get the ransom money for him.'

"Ali Riza hid until daytime. Then he walked and walked for hours along the shoreline until at last he came to a village. There were several fishing boats there, and Ali Riza persuaded one of the fishermen to take him to Salonica.

"There was still a long way to walk from the harbor to his mother's house. He rested overnight on the way, in a suburb of Salonica, and the peasants told him which road was safe to his village, Horhorsuyu. Finally he came home and rang the doorbell. And that, Mustafa, is the story of your father and the bandits."

Mustafa sighed happily. "What a brave man my father was! Some day I shall be like him."

Zübeyde smiled. "Yes, my son. Some day you will be like your father. Allah willing, you will be even bolder and braver than he was. Come, now, and go to bed. See, Makbule is sound asleep already."

50

"She is a girl," said Mustafa scornfully. "What do girls care for bravery? But for men like us it is different." And up the stairs he went, his head held high in memory of his father.

5

GOLDEN DAYS AT RAPLA

AT LAST it stopped raining. The mud dried hard, and the ground was firm. Surely now they could go outside to play. To their delight, their mother bundled them up warmly and allowed them to go out one wintry gray day to visit the hut. On their way they met Ismail, the son of Yavaşma, one of the farmhands. He had a pile of sticks on his back, and in his hand he carried a bucket in which there were some live coals.

"Please, Mustafa," he said. "I am *so* cold. Please let me build a little fire in your hut to warm myself."

Mustafa knew how cold it was, and he felt sorry for poor Ismail in his thin clothes. "Of course," he said. "But be very careful."

Ismail ran on ahead of them and built a little fire on the dirt floor of the hut. When they arrived, he was blowing on the ashes to make the sticks burn faster. Very quickly the hut filled with smoke. Alarmed, they all ran out. As they turned back to look, they saw that the straw matting covering the hut had caught fire and the whole hut was ablaze. The sight frightened Mustafa and Makbule. They stood close to each other and shivered with fear. They could not take their eyes off the burning hut. Makbule was crying, and Mustafa kept saying, "Don't cry, Makbush. I'll make you another one, much bigger and better than this one."

When they returned home, they met their mother. They could read in her eyes how angry she was. First she asked them where they had been, and they told her she had promised them they could go and see their hut.

"But you did not tell me you were going to build a fire there," she said crossly. "You played with fire and burned the hut, didn't you? Why did you do it? Tell me! You know that the storage room and the wood piles and the straw piles are all right close by. Praise Allah there was no wind! Even *you* could have caught on fire!"

"But, Mother, I didn't do it. Honestly I didn't. Just ask Makbush. *She* will tell you," said Mustafa. He had never seen his mother so angry before.

"Why should I ask Makbush? Only a few minutes ago, Ismail came in and told me all about it. You have deliberately set the hut on fire!"

Mustafa was shocked to hear his mother say that. He looked straight into his mother's eyes. "How could Ismail say such a thing, when he started the fire himself? Please, Mother, believe me. Ismail is telling a lie. He brought the sticks and he brought the coals. He told us he was cold, so we let him use our hut. Why would we want to burn down our own hut? And how could Ismail tell such a lie?"

At that moment Uncle Hüseyin entered the room. He had heard what Mustafa had said to his mother. He whispered something into Zübeyde's ear, and the two went into the next room. When they came back into the room, Mustafa did not even turn to look at them, he was so unhappy.

His uncle said, "Come to me, Mustafa, and tell me about it. I can see you are upset."

"I have nothing to tell, Uncle Hüseyin," Mustafa said. His lip trembled, but he refused to cry.

"Come here, my boy," his uncle said gently. "I know all about it. You had nothing to do with setting the fire. Ismail has no mother any more, only a stepmother who treats him very badly. Besides, he is not a very clever boy, you know. He has already started six fires on the farm, and he has always given the same excuse — that he was cold. He always tries to blame the fires on others. No matter how much I have talked with him, I cannot seem to make him change his ways."

Suddenly Mustafa could breathe freely again. He looked then at his uncle. "Thank you, Uncle Hüseyin. If you hadn't said these things, I don't think my mother would ever have believed me. And I want her to trust my word. You *do* believe me now, don't you, Mother?"

Zübeyde patted his shoulder and nodded, her eyes too full of tears for her to speak. This Mustafa, this boy of hers, was almost too much for her, at times. Praise be to Allah, he had a good uncle to take his father's place!

As for the hut, Mustafa kept his promise to Makbule and built another one, even bigger and better, and they spent many happy days in it. One day Uncle Hüseyin came out to visit them in the new hut. "This is such a fine house," he said. "Don't you think you need a watchdog to guard it?" His eyes twinkled as he spoke.

Mustafa was puzzled. A *watchdog* to guard his hut? What would a hut need of a watchdog?

"Come, Mustafa and Makbule," said their uncle. "I'll show you what I mean." He walked with them to the house where Ismail's parents lived. As he came close to

54

the house, he called, "Zilche! Zilche! I am bringing the children to you!" As their uncle called, the big farm watchdog came running out. At once she led them directly to the barn. When she opened the barn door with her nose, four puppies tumbled out. How surprised Mustafa and Makbule were! They squatted down to hug and pet the puppies.

"Well, Mustafa, *now* what do you think of a watchdog for your hut?" He looked from Mustafa to Makbule for an answer.

"Now I know what you meant by needing a watchdog," Mustafa answered. He nodded eagerly.

"But, Uncle Hüseyin," said Makbule, "one dog would not be enough. We need one to guard the hut in the daytime and another to guard it at night. One dog would be too sleepy to guard it all the time."

Their uncle was greatly pleased with little Makbule's reasoning, so they were allowed to choose two puppies to take home with them. They named one of the puppies Cin (Genie) and the other Alev (Flame). During the daytime the children played with the puppies, but just before dark they took them back to be with their mother, Zilche, in the barn. They loved their puppies, and the puppies soon grew used to them. Each puppy had its favorite food. Alev loved white cheese, and Cin loved sausages. Every morning before the children went to their hut to play, their mother always gave them two packages of food, one for them and one for their puppies.

Besides taking care of their puppies, the children were responsible for taking care of their uncle's favorite cat, Kuzgun (Blacky). One day Kuzgun had five kittens in the corner of Uncle Hüseyin's bedroom. How excited Mustafa and Makbule were when they found them, with the kittens so small their eyes were still tight shut. Their uncle cautioned them to keep the door to the hall tightly closed and to use the door into the next bedroom so no stray animal could get in to harm the new little kittens. Not once did they forget to use the right door. Every morning when the children woke up, the first things they thought of were the puppies and the kittens.

After this, the children began to look for other baby animals on the farm — the lambs, the calves, the baby water buffaloes, and the chicks. And everything they saw gave them fine new questions to ask, about how they were born, and what they ate, and where they slept. Truly, the children would have made good farmers.

One day Mustafa found a baby crow on the roof of the barn. It had fallen there out of its nest and was hurt. It could not fly. This made Mustafa unhappy. He had to help this crow. Yes, he had shot a bag full of crows while he was hunting with his uncle, but this one was different. This one was hurt and in pain. How it looked at Mustafa with its jet-black eyes and begged for help! Mustafa ran to his uncle. "Please, Uncle Hüseyin," he asked, "tell me what I should do with this crow."

"Do as you did with the others, Mustafa. What do you do with harmful animals?"

"You mean *kill* it, Uncle Hüseyin? No, I can't do that. You see, this one is different. This crow is hurt, and we must help him. Look how his mother is flying over us and crying!"

"But Mustafa, you killed a whole bag of crows when you went hunting with me."

"Yes, Uncle Hüseyin, I know that, but when they are flying up in the air they do not know you are going to shoot them. And when you shoot them and they fall down, they are dead. They don't feel anything. But look at this one suffer!"

"Then what are you going to do with it?" asked his uncle.

56

"I'm going to take care of him, and maybe one day he'll be well and can fly again."

"It is hard to take care of a crow, my boy. But suppose you *do* take care of him and he gets well and can fly again, then what will you do? Will you let him fly away?"

"Yes, Uncle, I will. I'll let him fly away. Birds are meant to be free."

There were several little sheds next to the barn. These had been used as guest rooms before, but for a long time no visitors had used them, and they were empty. His uncle gave Mustafa one of these rooms in which he could take care of his crow. As soon as Mustafa had put the crow inside the room, he hurried out to bring back an armful of branches so that the little bird would feel at home. After a few days, Mustafa said to his sister, "Come, Makbush. I have a surprise for you. Go to our hut and wait there for me."

Makbule hurried to the hut and waited, wondering what Mustafa might be planning. Mustafa meanwhile ran to the little room where the crow lived, and came over to the hut with the baby crow perched on his arm. When he saw Makbule, he tossed the bird toward the cherry tree beside the hut. Then he called, "Come, Hacı!" The bird flew back and sat on his arm.

"Oh, Mustafa, he is well!" cried Makbule. "You were right. He *did* learn to fly, after all. And Hacı ("Pilgrim") is a good name for him. He comes to you as a good pilgrim goes to Mecca." And indeed Hacı did fly to Mustafa whenever Mustafa called.

The days passed swiftly and happily for Mustafa and Makbule at Rapla, but Zübeyde thought incessantly of a good education for her son. He was growing up a peasant, she feared. How could he ever become the man she had envisioned? At last she took the only step within her means. She wrote to her aunt Hatice in Salonica, and asked if she would keep Mustafa at her home during the week while he attended school. He would return to Rapla for the holy day each week, since he was still a young child, only eleven, and needed some time with his own family. After some delay, Hatice responded that she would certainly provide a home for Mustafa in Salonica.

As soon as she had read Hatice's letter, Zübeyde called her son from the field where he and Makbule were guarding the horsebeans against the crows. "Mustafa," she said, her eyes shining with the delight of it, "your great-aunt Hatice has written to say you may live with her in Salonica and go to school. What do you think of that?"

Mustafa furrowed his brow. In truth, he did not know what to think of it. He had become thoroughly adapted to farm life, and loved the days there. On the other hand, he was parched to *know*, and there was little more that he could learn at Rapla. He well knew that life would not be easy in Salonica at the hands of his great-aunt Hatice. She and his mother had never been on good terms, and he had rarely visited there. She was a stern and demanding person, with not a scrap of humor in her. Of all his relatives, she had the least sympathy with this restless dreamer and doer. Could he bear her harsh ways?

Suddenly Mustafa knew. "Mother," he said, "I want to *be* somebody. To be somebody, I must go to school. Yes, I shall go to my great-aunt in Salonica. But how often can I come to Rapla? Now that I have lived here, I cannot leave it altogether."

"Of course you may come to Rapla," his mother answered, relieved that he had agreed to return to school. "Your uncle has a foal for you in his stable. Every Thursday noon after school you may ride home to Rapla to spend Thursday afternoon and Friday. Then of course you will return to Salonica for school on Saturday." (Thursday afternoon and all day Friday were school holidays. School was held on the other days of the week.)

When the day came for Mustafa to go to Salonica, the leave-taking was almost too much to bear. How could he leave the green, open fields, the freedom of those undisciplined days, for the demands of school and of life with his great-aunt Hatice? It was hard, too, to leave Makbule, and Kuzgun and her kittens, and Cin and Alev, and Hacı — yes, especially Hacı. And the hut in which he and Makbule had shared so many happy times — now Naciye, that young sister who did nothing but tease him and quarrel with him, would take his place with Makbule. Almost, Mustafa regretted his decision to go to Salonica ...

At least, he could visit the hut once more. For that one day, it would still be his. "Come, Makbule," he said. "I want to look once more at our hut." And he set off across the field, the sweet smell of the grasses in the field tickling his nose. Suddenly, when they were almost there, he changed his course. He would say goodbye to Hacı. And Makbule obediently ran with him to the little room next to the barn.

As they came nearer, they saw that the window was broken. "Hacı! Hacı!" Mustafa called, but there was no answering flutter of wings. They burst in through the door and searched feverishly through the branches, but Hacı was nowhere there.

"Perhaps he has flown to the hut," suggested Makbule, and they ran there to look. There was a cool breeze in the air, and as they were running they saw feathers caught up in the breeze. The children saw the feathers, but they refused to believe that the feathers were Hacı's.

"Hacı! Hacı!" Mustafa called, his voice hoarse from anxiety. But Hacı did not fly to perch on his arm. As they looked about, they saw more and more feathers. Mak-

59

bule caught one and looked at it, not wanting to believe what she saw. Then she said softly, "Mustafa, this is Hacı's feather."

Mustafa, still unbelieving, picked up a small handful of feathers and looked at them closely. Yes, they were Hacı's feathers. His eyes filled with tears, Mustafa looked for the torn body of his crow. At the corner of the hut they found Hacı, still, the blood caked against wings which would never fly again. The two stood there for a moment, looking down at that small proud thing, now humbled. Then Mustafa spoke, his voice ragged with grief. "We must bury him here, where he fell." And they dug a small grave and buried Hacı.

"How did it happen, Mustafa?" asked Makbule, as desolate as he about the crow's death. Relieved to have something to do, they set forth to find out. The trail was all too plain to see. The wild bull in the west field had broken loose and had smashed the window of the little room with his horn. Hacı had flown out to the hut, where he had gone so often with the children. There the sheep dog had found him and killed him.

"Uncle Hüseyin, Hacı is dead," Mustafa said as his uncle came close to see what was troubling the children. "Please plant a tree here, where we have laid him. It will bloom in memory of Hacı. I will then have something alive for mine in place of my little dead crow."

And, true enough, a mulberry tree was planted there, a tree the whole family called the Hacı tree.

6

MUSTAFA FINDS A WAY

ZÜBEYDE had had many second thoughts about Mustafa and his life in Salonica with his great-aunt. Mustafa did not talk about Hatice at all when he came to spend his holidays at Rapla. But the feverish way in which he threw himself into these few hours on the farm made his mother suspect that matters were not going well between Mustafa and Hatice. Hatice's letters were few, and gave no satisfaction. At last Zübeyde had to find out for herself. Since she and Hatice did not get along at all well, Zübeyde asked Hüseyin to stop in at Hatice's house the next time he went to Salonica on business, and Hüseyin agreed to make the visit.

It took but half an hour for him to discover that Mustafa was bitterly unhappy with his great-aunt. Hatice was a willful and capricious woman. As soon as Hüseyin had arrived, she called sharply, "Mustafa! Go out and get me a *simit.*"

Out into the rain went Mustafa, his face set and his shoulders back. While he was gone, they discussed matters on the farm, and the way in which things stood between Hatice and Mustafa. The boy gave no satisfaction, she felt. He was unruly and unrespectful, altogether too much for an old woman to tolerate.

At that moment the boy came in, a fresh pretzel held carefully in his hand. "Here you are, Great-Aunt Hatice," he said, his voice low and polite, but a stiffness in his shoulders betrayed his pride and assurance.

"It is wet!" she exclaimed, and she tossed it aside.

"It is raining outside, Great-Aunt Hatice. I protected it as well as I could."

"There is *always* something wrong!" she said irritably. "You see, Hüseyin? The boy is impossible!"

Hüseyin nodded. "I can see that he irritates you," he said politely. But there was no question in his mind about who might be at the root of the irritation. He rose to go. "I shall carry Zübeyde your greetings," he said. And he left.

Indeed, the boy must be *determined* to finish his schooling, he thought as he returned to Rapla. He is a proud child, and he dislikes being ordered about. Nevertheless, he did as she demanded. There seemed to be no way in which he could satisfy her. It was clearly too much for him.

"Mustafa is a quiet boy, and he is very sensitive," Hüseyin told Zübeyde on his return from Salonica. "He has kept quiet about all these irritations. He was unwilling to say much even when I asked him about it. He said only that he does not wish to live with his great-aunt. He has left the decision to us."

When Mustafa's grandmother heard this, she insisted, "We cannot leave the boy there any longer."

62

Turning to Zübeyde, she said, "Either you or I must go to Salonica to make a home for the boy."

Since Zübeyde was unable to leave the farm with her two young daughters, it was decided that the grandmother would go. The big house in which Mustafa had lived with his parents had been rented, so they must find another house. Luckily, there was a small house for rent in the same neighborhood, so Mustafa's grandmother moved there with her household goods, and Mustafa, to his great relief, came to live with his grandmother.

The school that Mustafa attended was not as modern and as stimulating as Şemsi Efendi's school had been. The schoolmasters there were harsh and unsympathetic, and believed strongly in beating boys to encourage them to learn. One of the masters in this school was Kaymak Hafız (*Kaymak* means "whipped cream"), and the boys in the school, knowing their master's fondness for whipped cream, had nicknamed him "Slushy." Certain other traits about Kaymak Hafız aroused comment among the students: he used mascara on his eyes, and he wore ornate and excessively decorated clothing. For some reason, this particular master took an immediate dislike to Mustafa — perhaps because he was a proud, silent boy who resented punishment. For quite some time, Mustafa managed to get along with Kaymak Hafız, despite his distaste for the master's cruel methods. (The presence in the school of one of Mustafa's earlier neighbors, Mehmet Somer, now his classmate, may well have helped to ease the stress of his learning under such pressure.) But one day during a class taught by Kaymak Hafız, Mustafa fell into a quarrel and then a fistfight with another of his classmates over some rather trifling matter, an incident that provided exactly the opening that Kaymak Hafız had been looking for. He beat Mustafa mercilessly. Crying with pain and rage,

Mustafa left the school and went home.

His grandmother heard him coming, and went to the door to meet him. When she saw the boy all bruised and bleeding, she asked him what had happened. Mustafa told her the whole story, determined that she should know the truth about Kaymak Hafız and his ways with his students. His grandmother, who loved Mustafa dearly, decided that Mustafa would not return to that school. After she had treated Mustafa's cuts and bruises, she went directly to a public scribe to have a letter written to Zübeyde about the matter.

As for Mustafa, he was troubled about being taken out of school, even Kaymak Hafız's school. Time after time, his education had been interrupted. How would he ever get to *be* somebody? Surely some way could be found for him to learn those things which he needed to know.

Uncle Hüseyin thought he knew the answer. "You must send him to a military school," he said. "Mustafa is clever, but he is headstrong and quite undisciplined. He will benefit by being brought under strict control. You know how I love the boy, even as you love him. But you must confess he is difficult to manage."

Zübeyde knew that fact only too well. All too often had she and her strong-willed son came to angry words over a decision that must be made. But a military school! That would mean that Mustafa would be trained to become an officer. And no officer's life was safe. Although Sultan Abdul Hamid provided a free education for his army officers, he trusted not a single one of them. He had a spy listening in on every conversation, seeking news of plots against his life. No, Mustafa must not become an officer. That was not the kind of future she had in mind for her son.

Hüseyin continued to urge Zübeyde to consider a military school for Mustafa. "He will get a good education. His schooling will cost you nothing. If Mustafa has outstanding ability, he will become an officer. If he is stubborn and does not do well, he will become merely a private. At any rate, he will have found something useful to do. Surely he cannot continue in this hit-or-miss fashion." But Zübeyde still could not accept this solution.

Meanwhile, Mustafa had been doing some thinking of his own. In their neighborhood lived an old friend of his father's, Major Kadri Bey, who had long been an officer in the Sultan's army. Kadri Bey had a son Ahmed who was presently attending the Askeri Rüştiye (military secondary school). Every morning Ahmed swaggered down the cobblestone streets to school, trim in his military uniform with its shiny buttons. Mustafa could imagine himself in just such a uniform, going forth to get the education which he so sorely wanted. How fine it would be to become a soldier!

At this time, Zübeyde returned to Salonica, where she bought a house for her family. She remarried shortly afterwards, a native of Rhodes named Ragıp Bey who had come from Larisa to Salonica and who served in the Customs Administration. Ragıp Bey came to live in Zübeyde's house, and Mustafa, who had planned to live with his mother and sisters, went instead to another quarter of Salonica to live with his aunt Emine, a sister of Ali Riza. He continued to live with his aunt until he went to military boarding school in Monastır.

Mustafa was bitter and resentful about his mother's remarriage, and refused even to exchange words with his stepfather. But his stepfather's son Süreya, himself an officer, undertook to win Mustafa over. At length Mustafa came to respect Ragıp Bey and to accept this new relationship, although Ragıp Bey never replaced Ali Riza in Mustafa's life, nor did his decisions carry any weight with the boy.

Mustafa himself approached his mother on the

matter of a military school. "The Sultan himself sees to the officers' education, Mother. In the military school I would really have a chance to *be* somebody. Every boy has an equal chance to rise in the military. I should there be the equal of any *paşa*'s son."

But Zübeyde would not listen to the boy. "I want you to become a respected man, a *hoca*, my boy. You are clever, and you will make a fine teacher. I cannot allow you to become a soldier."

"Mother," said Mustafa, his eyes bright, "do you remember what was hanging above my cradle as I was named? You have told me about it many times yourself. Yes, it was my father's sword, curved and shining and with a proud history. Surely my father would have wanted me to become a soldier!" Even as he spoke, Mustafa watched his mother's face. Her jaw stiffened, and she formed her mouth to tell him "No" again. Well, he would manage the matter by himself.

One day, Mustafa disappeared from his aunt's house, and no amount of calling could bring him in. He had talked long and earnestly with Ahmed and Major Kadri Bey and had found out what he must do to obtain admission to the military school. He must sit for a series of examinations. Well, sit for them he would. It was on this day, then, that he had gone to the military school, entirely without his mother's knowledge or permission. After all, he thought, a man must look out for himself in this world.

After he had finished the examinations, he waited outside the gate for the examiners' decision. At length the door opened and the supervising officer appeared, calling, "Mustafa! Mustafa Efendi!" Mustafa had heard this officer, who served also as the physical education teacher in the military school.

"Sir!" Mustafa responded respectfully, and he stood at attention, as he had seen soldiers do.

"I congratulate you, my boy," said the officer. "You wrote a brilliant examination, and you have been accepted into the third class of our school."

Think of that! Mustafa had applied for admission to the second class, and he had done so well in the examinations that he had become a third-year student! That was not too bad for a twelve-year-old. . . . Well, he would prove to them that they had made the right decision.

As soon as the officer had gone inside and shut the door, Mustafa ran to his mother's house, "third class . . . third class . . . third class" still ringing in his head. "Mother! Mother!" he called as he burst into the house.

Zübeyde, half frantic with worry over her son's disappearance from his aunt's house, scarcely knew what to make of Mustafa's excitement. "Tell me, my son," she said. "Where were you?"

"At school, Mother."

"*What* school?"

"The military academy, Mother."

"Mustafa! What were you doing there?"

"I took my examinations, Mother."

"Examinations? What examinations?"

"Entrance examinations, Mother. And I have been accepted into the third class. Think of that!"

Zübeyde watched her excited son. Clearly he was happier than he had been for many months, ever since he had left the farm. Was she right to oppose his determination to become a soldier, perhaps an officer? Zübeyde studied her son quietly, his blond hair awry from running, his blue-grey eyes shining with pride and triumph, his shoulders thrown back. Then she knew what she must do. She put her hands on his shoulders, and her blue-grey eyes looked steadily into his. "Good luck, my son. May Allah be with you. And may you do great service for your country."

"Mother," said the boy, relieved and proud that his mother had accepted his decision, "Some day you will be proud of me. I promise you that."

Thus Mustafa's goal was set. What would become of it, and of him, could only be decided by time. But from this day forth, Zübeyde accepted her son's goal as her own. Whatever sacrifices must be made to reach that goal she was prepared to face.

Mustafa fell into the new way of life readily and comfortably. He found his classes challenging and his teachers stimulating. Mathematics was his favorite subject, as indeed it had always been, and for that class he had a fine teacher himself named Mustafa. Quickly Zübeyde's son came into a position of leadership in the class. The teacher had developed a method of teaching in which he used junior teachers or monitors to teach the slower students. Very quickly young Mustafa showed his ability in mathematics, and he was chosen to be the discussion tutor. Of course, he enjoyed the prestige which his new position gave him among the boys. At the end of the first three months he passed his examinations and was issued his first uniform. How he swaggered as he wore it!

It was a handsome uniform, navy blue, with a jacket fitted snugly at the waist and a row of shiny gold buttons, each bearing the Turkish star and crescent, marching down the front. On the jacket sleeve there were three rows of green ribbon half an inch in width, one row representing each class year. The trousers were narrow and had a stripe of green ribbon down the side. On his head he wore a bright red fez with a black tassel, slightly pulled down over his left eyebrow. Yes, it was fine dress for a handsome boy, of slim, athletic build, with strong arms and long, thin fingers. He looked taller than he was, for he had a proud stance about him. With his blond hair, fair skin, and bold blue eyes he cut a striking figure.

Mustafa wore his uniform that first day to visit his mother and his sisters at his mother's house, While he was there, Uncle Hüseyin came, bringing a large pot of yoghurt from Rapla. Putting it down on the kitchen table, Hüseyin went back into the living room to talk with Zübeyde.

As soon as Mustafa and Makbule and Naciye heard their uncle talking, they scurried into the kitchen to see what good things he had brought from the farm. "Yoghurt!" whispered Makbule, dipping her finger into the pot a little bit to see how good it tasted. Naciye looked at Mustafa, so dignified in his blue uniform, and then she too dipped a finger into the yoghurt and popped it into her mouth.

Mustafa watched them for a moment, and then he had an idea. His eyes twinkled. He loved a practical joke, and here was a good chance to play one.

"Shame on you, Makbule!" he said. "Can't you eat yoghurt any faster than that? Go ahead! Put your face into the pot and use your tongue. You can eat much faster that way."

Now that Mustafa had suggested it, this sounded like a good idea to Makbule. Putting her face down into the pot, she began to lick the yoghurt with her tongue. Suddenly Mustafa gave her head a little push, and *Schlish*! her whole face went into the yoghurt. Naciye giggled and gave Makbule's braid a tweak to duck her face again into the yoghurt.

"Now you look exactly like a clown!" Mustafa crowed. They were all laughing so hard that they did not hear Hüseyin and Zübeyde come into the kitchen.

"Well," said Uncle Hüseyin, laughing in spite of himself at Makbule, smeared from forehead to chin with yoghurt. "You certainly know how to enjoy yoghurt!" Then, turning to Zübeyde, he said, "I suspect Master Mustafa's hand in this. With all the growing pains he has,

I'm glad to see that he still keeps his sense of fun."

And indeed Mustafa had a sense of fun. He and Naciye were well matched in that respect. She well knew Mustafa's horror of rats. For this reason, one Thursday evening at Rapla while Mustafa was home from Salonica for the holy day, she had come running into the living room.

"Mustafa!" she whispered loudly. "I just saw a rat run into your bedroom. It was a *lovely* gray rat with a long, long tail and long whiskers. How it squeaked! It ran under your bed, and I shut your door to keep it there for you," Her eyes danced as she waited for his response.

Mustafa's stomach churned. "Mother," he said, "I don't feel like sleeping in my own room tonight. Please let me sleep somewhere else — perhaps on the small bed in Uncle Hüseyin's room."

Zübeyde, who had been smiling at Naciye's teasing of her brother, was suddenly irritated. "What a silly you are!" she exclaimed. "You talk often about becoming a brave soldier. Yet here you are, timid about a rat!"

"I'm not *timid* about them. I just don't *like* them," Mustafa returned. "Rats bite your ears when you're asleep."

But his answer hadn't convinced anyone. Long after that time, on Thursday evenings when Mustafa was studying in his room on the farm, Naciye had crept up to his door and scratched and squeaked, very like a rat, to tease this big brother who seemed to be so brave about everything else except rats. It was only fair return, she thought, for the tricks he was always playing on her.

"This time, the joke was on Makbule," Zübeyde said. "Run along, now, and wash your face. And Mustafa, you may come and talk with us. Uncle Hüseyin wants to hear about your work at school." And Mustafa went on into the living room with his mother and his uncle, only too pleased to talk about his studies at Rüştiye.

70

Mustafa performed well in all his classes, and won his teachers' respect and admiration for the penetrating questions that he asked. More than all the others, he was eager to learn. Captain Mustafa, his mathematics teacher, called him to his desk after class one day. "Mustafa," he said, "you and I share the same name. I think there should be some distinction between us. From now on, I shall call you Mustafa Kemal" (*Kemal* means "perfection").

That afternoon Mustafa went directly to his mother's house after school. "Guess what, Mother?" he asked as he found her in the kitchen. "I have a new name."

"What was wrong with the name *Mustafa?*" his mother asked, puzzled. "Your father chose that name for you, and it has always been good enough for you before."

"Oh, Mother, you do not understand! I am not changing the name my father gave me. But today Captain Mustafa added another name to it. There is nothing wrong with two names, is there? My father had two names — *Ali Riza.*"

"What business has your teacher giving you another name?"

"Today in our mathematics class he asked a very difficult problem. I solved it quickly and correctly. This pleased the teacher very much, so he gave me the name *Kemal.* He said that since we were both named *Mustafa,* there should be some distinction between us. Now my name is Mustafa Kemal!"

"It is a fine, proud name, my son. May it bring you good luck and many blessings," she said.

"When I am a *paşa,* Mother, they'll call me Mustafa Kemal Paşa, and you will be known as the mother of Mustafa Kemal Paşa!"

From that day forth, Mustafa was known as Mustafa Kemal.

That year, Mustafa Kemal was chosen president of his class. Though he was a close friend of few boys in his class — he was too reserved and silent to encourage the banter and easy intimacy of his fellows — Zübeyde's son had won their respect and admiration. He had developed a sound sense of his own goals and his desire for prestige, and this gave him an air of leadership which overshadowed that of more popular boys.

Shortly before he was fourteen, Mustafa Kemal fell in love with a young girl in his neighborhood. He was of course not allowed to speak with her — after the age of nine or ten no nice girl was seen talking with a boy — but he could watch her at a distance, and so he did. As soon as he arrived home in the afternoon, he had his trousers neatly pressed and then he hurried forth in his handsome uniform to parade back and forth past his sweetheart's window with the hope of catching a glimpse at her behind the shutter. Unfortunately, he was never able to get to know her beyond this slight connection.

Mustafa Kemal finished his work at the military secondary school in 1895, graduating with honors. The following fall, at the age of fourteen, he was enrolled at the military boarding school (high school) in a town in central Macedonia named Monastır (Ali Riza's birthplace, now Bitola, in southern Yugoslavia); his student number there was 7348. (All the students there were identified and addressed only by number; they kept the same number as long as they remained students at that school.) Three of his friends from Rüştiye Military School went with him as students to Monastır. In addition to these three, he was close to Ömer Naci, who had been expelled from the Bursa military school and then sent to Monastır.

Ömer was at first a great puzzle to Mustafa Kemal because he wished to spend all his time reading books of poetry and other literature. Mustafa Kemal throughout his years in school had always been so concerned with mathematics that he had had small interest in other subjects. Ömer came again and again to Mustafa Kemal's room to borrow books, and each time he returned them he said that he had not liked them. Mustafa Kemal became very curious about the kinds of books that Ömer *did* like to read. Gradually Ömer opened up to him a world that he had never known, the world of literature. He discovered poetry, and found that he liked to write it. He found expressed in poetry — especially the poetry of Namık Kemal — many of the thoughts that for years had lain at the back of his head, thoughts about love of country and patriotism and freedom of thought and political freedom. Gradually his interest in poetry became known to his composition teacher. This teacher called Mustafa Kemal to him one day. "My boy," he said, "you are spending entirely too much time in reading and writing poetry. You will never become a good soldier if you spend your leisure hours in this way."

Mustafa Kemal thought again and again about what the teacher had said. There might, after all, be some truth to it. On the other hand, there was much to be said for strong and powerful expression of ideas. At last he decided that he would lay aside the poetry for a while, but that he would never cease to be interested in writing and speaking well. He continued to read whatever he could find of fine writing, and to discuss what he read with another of his close friends, Ali Fethi.

A bout of malaria while Mustafa Kemal was at Monastır cost him two months of school. When Zübeyde learned that her son was ill, she herself traveled to Monastır to see the chief doctor at the school, Dr. Muhsin Bey. "I sent you a healthy boy," she said, "and just look at him now!" She insisted on taking him home to Salonica to nurse him back to health. Mustafa Kemal was very, very thin and weak from successive attacks of fever and severe shaking spells. But after two months of care by Zübeyde, he had recovered and was able to return to school.

While Mustafa Kemal was a student at Monastır, he had to take a subject which was new and difficult for him; he had to master French as a foreign language. No matter how hard he worked on this subject, his tongue would trip him up, until finally his French teacher warned him that he was likely to fail the course. That summer while Mustafa Kemal was on vacation for three months in Salonica, he went regularly, but in secret, to the Dominican Brothers' school, and there he finally managed to learn the language well enough so that he no longer had to worry about it as a subject in school. As he continued to grow and to read, he discovered that many of the Western ideas which interested him most were written in French books, and thus he continued to read French long past the time when he was required to know it.

During the time that Mustafa Kemal was a student in Monastır, something happened which excited the hearts of all Turks, but especially of those in military schools. There was increased strife between the Greeks and the Turks, who had traditionally been enemies in Macedonia. Greece had seized Crete, and Turkey had thereupon declared war on Greece. Turkish men and boys were eagerly volunteering to serve their country. Off they would go to war, with Turkish flags in their hands, marching to the music of the *zurna* (a native Turkish oboe) and the drum.

Mustafa Kemal had been watching the trouble between the Greeks and the Turks as it worsened. There grew in his heart a strong desire to serve his country in its time of trouble. What better way was there to serve than to go off to war? Secretly he and a good friend of his planned to run away from the military school in Monastır and enlist for military service.

74

He and his friend looked all that day for a group of volunteers that they could join, but no one seemed to have time for them. Finally night came, and they realized that they would have to find a place to stay. Mustafa Kemal boldly went up to the door of a house and knocked. When a woman came to the door, he asked, "Madam, will you accept two guests for the night?"

Saying nothing, the woman brought a kerosene lamp so that she could see their faces. "Why, Mustafa!" she said. "What are you doing here?"

As it happened, she was a Bulgarian woman who had lived in Salonica and knew Zübeyde. She invited the boys inside, and then she asked, "Where are you going, Mustafa?"

"I am going to the battlefront, Ma'am, and I am going to fight against the Greeks," he said proudly.

"My boys," she answered, "you are both brave to want to fight for your country. But in times like these, your country needs soldiers who are well trained. I can see by your uniforms that you are military high school students. When you have finished your training, your country will have great need of you. But first you must finish your training."

Mustafa Kemal and his friend stood for a moment, thinking of what she had said. Then they looked at one another. "You are right, Ma'am," said Mustafa Kemal. "We must return to our work at school. When we are ready, our country will be ready for us." And the two boys returned to the Monastır military school, to the work that would prepare them even better than they knew for service to their country.

Mustafa Kemal completed his three years of study at Monastır İdadisi and graduated with honors at the age of eighteen in March of 1899. It was clear now not only to the boy himself but to his family that he was destined to become a military officer, so he was entered that fall as a member of the infantry class of Harbiye (War College) in Istanbul (called by Westerners Constantinople), with his school number being 1283; he kept this number throughout the three years he attended Harbiye.

Mustafa had never before lived in a city as big or as varied as Istanbul. For the whole first year he was there, he explored the city and learned from all its sights and sounds. It was here that he first became acquainted, as did the other students at the War College, with city night life — with dancing girls and taverns and music halls that would be certain to attract boys from small towns. At first a stranger and alone, he soon found a close friend and companion in Ali Fuad, a member of an aristocratic family living in Istanbul. Ali Fuad's relatives found Mustafa Kemal agreeable company, and he became almost a member of the family. At the suggestion of Ali Fuad's father, a military general, they mapped the entire city, coming to know it very well indeed. With such pleasant diversions, that whole first year had passed before Mustafa Kemal remembered that he had come to Istanbul to study for becoming an officer. But all that he had learned during that first year would later come to play a leading part in his life.

The following year, he plunged into college work, determined to establish a record there as a good student. During this second year, Mustafa Kemal began to learn much of politics, and to be aware that Turkey was in fully as much danger from corruption within as from attacks by its outside enemies. During his free hours at the college, he and his friends would meet for contests in oratory, in public speaking, debating long and hotly the evidences of corruption within the Ottoman Empire and the international problems which beset Turkey. In these debates, Mustafa was concerned for major and drastic changes, while the others, coming from more conservative backgrounds, favored moderate reforms in the present system.. These debating sessions forced Mustafa Kemal to think about his country and its problems more deeply than he had ever thought before. And at the back of his mind began to stir a strange and wild and wonderful idea — that he might be able some day to set the people of his country free, even as he had set free those two goldfinches in the market at Salonica.

Gradually he began to read more and more history, to study the ways in which political changes could be managed, to understand the ways in which men's minds could be directed. After graduation in 1902 from Harbiye as a lieutenant (ranking eighth highest in his class), he went on to the General Staff College. There he wrestled with problems of military tactics, learning how to conduct battles and to wage wars. Here his mind was first intrigued by the idea of guerrilla warfare, a kind of warfare his teacher of tactics, Nuri Bey of Trabzon, claimed was as difficult to repress as it was to organize. Excited by this possibility, Mustafa Kemal asked for a special assignment: to be allowed to map out a guerrilla war against Turkey. Curiously enough, it was just this kind of military planning which later enabled him to lead his country to victory against its enemies.

While he was a student at the General Staff College, Mustafa Kemal and his friends decided to publish and circulate a handwritten newspaper warning their classmates of the corruption within the Ottoman Empire and urging them to listen to the new ideas of freedom and democracy from the West. They formed a branch of the secret society called the *Vatan* ("Fatherland"). They read all kinds of forbidden books, argued all kinds of ideas, and created for themselves a great deal of trouble. For the Sultan was all too well aware of the corruption within his realm, and he was determined to stamp out any opposition to it. All those who taught in the military schools were to spy out for him the hotheads who spoke against his policies. Therefore, İsmail Paşa, the Inspector-General of the Institutes for Military Training, reported to the palace that a student newspaper at the General Staff College was inciting rebellion against the Sultan, Abdul Hamid.

One evening while Mustafa Kemal and his friends were gathered in the veterinary college to put together an issue of the newspaper, the door burst open and they were discovered. The principal of the school, Riza Paşa, fearful of losing his post as principal, did not report what he had discovered. He merely warned the students that they must attend only to their studies. From that time on, the students were more careful than ever in publishing their newspaper. Someday the axe would fall, and one or more of them would suffer. Well, then, let it fall. The fate of Turkey was more important than the fate of any single officer or group of officers.

During these days, Mustafa Kemal's heart was restless, and his head was incessantly busy with problems of politics and of history. His mind played also with problems of tactics. He would smuggle forbidden books into his room, and read them for hours at night, under the bed covers, in the poor light that could be managed there. Often he would be awake the rest of the night puzzling out some problem or another. He would fall asleep just before daybreak, and when the guard officer came to awaken him he would be sulky and sleepy. Still, half asleep though he looked, he would be the first to answer a difficult question in class. This puzzling, planning student was laying the groundwork for leadership, the kind of leadership that would make Turkey a new, free nation, with its eyes toward Europe and America rather than toward the Orient.

In January of 1905, when he was barely twenty-four, Mustafa Kemal was graduated from the General Staff College as a captain; he ranked fifth (several sources say

78

fourth) highest in his class. After graduation, he and his friends — Ali Fuad, Ali Fethi, Hüseyin Rauf, and Refet — rented a house in the Şişli quarter of Istanbul. There they met in secret to discuss politics and to decide what they might do to free Turkey from the grasp of the Sultan, to make it a proud, democratic nation. These ideas were not new to them. Many men before them had sought the same goal for Turkey, and they had been spied upon and then exiled. But these young men were different. They had been given the finest education that was available in Turkey, at the Ottoman Empire's expense. They knew full well what a tragic situation their nation was facing. And they had the will and the training to bring about a change.

One day a new man, Fethi Bey, came to join their discussions. "I have been expelled from military college," he said, "and I have nowhere else to go. Please let me stay here with you."

He was a minor military officer, and Mustafa Kemal took him in and provided for him. Too late, they discovered that he was a spy. To the palace guards he had reported what men were involved in Mustafa Kemal's group, how and where they met, and what matters they discussed in their meetings.

Suddenly the men were all arrested. As the leader of the group, Mustafa Kemal was taken to the palace for questioning. At length they were all imprisoned, awaiting the Sultan's decision as to what should be done with such traitors. Little by little, charges were dismissed against the others and they were released — all except Mustafa Kemal.

Week after week he waited in the Yıldız Palas Prison, the dreaded Red Prison (so called because of the color of its bricks) from which few men had returned. Zübeyde and Makbule came to Istanbul to visit him, but they were refused permission to see him. What was to become of him, of his dreams for his own future as a leader of his people?

At last a representative came from the Sultan himself. He assured Mustafa Kemal that he could have a brilliant future as an officer in the service of the Sultan. Unfortunately, he had disgraced his uniform in plotting against Abdul Hamid. But, the representative went on, the Sultan had decided this time to be merciful — that Mustafa Kemal was doubtless wild and headstrong, but not actually bad. The Sultan had decided to send Mustafa Kemal to join a cavalry regiment in Damascus. There he would be less able to plot mischief against the Sultan. And there he would be given an opportunity to show whether or not he had the makings of a fine officer in the Turkish army.

That night Mustafa Kemal was placed aboard a vessel for Beirut, bound overland then for Damascus, far distant from the scene on which he had hoped to find himself a leader. Who would guess that from such a beginning — in effect, an *exile* — Mustafa Kemal would one day become the savior of his country?

Yet in this boy Mustafa and this young man Mustafa Kemal had lain all the seeds of greatness which came to flower in the soldier-statesman Mustafa Kemal Atatürk.

Mustafa Kemal with his mother, Zübeyde Hanım, and his sister, Makbule.

Mustafa Kemal in trenches with soldiers at start of War of Dardanelles
(1915).

stafa Kemal as Commander of Derna in the Tripolitanian War
1).

The Great National Assembly at work before the heroic defense of Turkey against postwar partition by the Allies.

The Turkish Grand National Assembly, Ulus, Ankara (now used as a museum, Türk Inkilap Müsesi).

Mustafa Kemal with his wife, Latife.

Headquarters of camel drivers. At that time (the defense of Turkey against partition), all available transport had been solicited. The unselfish camel owners were the first to volunteer.

Mustafa Kemal, the Great Chief, teaching the new Turkish alphabet.

Atatürk's work desk in his home in Çankaya, Ankara. The picture on the desk is of his mother.

AFTERWORD

WHATEVER A MAN BECOMES is most often the fruit of seeds present in his childhood and his youth. For this reason it is good to discover what a great man was like, and what he experienced, in his early years. But unless we have at least an *idea* of the accomplishments of the mature man, it is a matter of little more than idle interest what he was in his youth.

Mustafa Kemal Atatürk, born into a rather ordinary family, proved to be a most extraordinary man. Many books have been written showing what Atatürk the man was like (or what the authors *thought* he was like) and what he did that seemed significant. Here we can give only a brief sketch of his achievements. But even a hint of these accomplishments will show how much of the man was in the boy you have met in this book.

81

* * * *

Mustafa Kemal, a well-trained military officer determined to serve the best interests of his country as he understood them, turned what had been intended by Sultan Abdul Hamid as near-exile into a priceless learning experience. In Damascus, the young captain observed at first hand the abuses practiced against its subject peoples — in this instance, the Druses — by the old Ottoman army. His effort to develop a new, efficient, honest kind of soldier for the Turkish army and to build among his men a sense of pride and military discipline was begun in Damascus and — over a period of fourteen years' work in Syria and elsewhere — was to prove the salvation of his country.

Too, he learned something highly significant from the sleepy, backward city of Damascus itself: its inhabitants, with no ambition for improving either themselves or their situation, left all progress in the hands of Allah. In sharp contrast to these Damascans were the Westerners — Italians — who had come there to work on the railroad. Accustomed to taking a hand in their own advancement, these Italians reflected the bustling European cultures about which Mustafa Kemal had read, and their energetic attitude strengthened the young captain's desire to bring Western-style progress to Turkey.

In Damascus there were several men who felt as Mustafa Kemal did about the corruption in the Ottoman government and about the need for drastic change. In 1906 they formed a secret organization called *Vatan ve Hürriyet* ("Fatherland and Freedom") to unite those men opposed to Ottoman abuses of power; little by little, branches of this organization were formed also in Beirut, Jaffa, and Jerusalem. But these groups were too far away from Istanbul to be helpful in changing the Ottoman pattern, Mustafa Kemal realized. Somehow he himself must get back to Salonica, where there were more people ready for revolt against the Sultan's despotism. He persuaded a superior officer in Jaffa to sign a false pass for him to Macedonia, and returned secretly by a roundabout route to Salonica. There he organized a branch of *Vatan ve Hürriyet* to plot a revolution against Abdul Hamid. When at last the Sultan's spies discovered that Mustafa Kemal was in Salonica, he hurried back to Jaffa and then onward to the Egyptian front. On questioning, the officer who had signed his pass responded that the Mustafa Kemal under his supervision had been on duty on the Egyptian front all the time. Surely that must have been some other Mustafa that they had seen in Salonica . . .

Finally, in 1907, Mustafa Kemal's exemplary military service in Syria in subduing the Druse revolt was recognized: no longer suspected by the Sultan, Mustafa Kemal was promoted to adjutant-major and assigned to Macedonia. There he served on the General Staff headquartered in Salonica. He continued to work effectively but discreetly with the *Vatan ve Hürriyet* organization, which was subsequently absorbed by the Committee for Union and Progress (its members gained the name "Young Turks"); too, he participated in the 1908 revolution requiring the Sultan to restore the Constitution. But the one credited as the leader of the Young Turks' Revolution was not Mustafa Kemal; another young army officer, his age-mate, Enver Bey, reaped public praise for that daring feat and thus moved rapidly toward the position of national leadership that Mustafa Kemal longed to have. Clearly, Mustafa Kemal's route to leadership must lie in even greater military accomplishments, so the young adjutant-general bent his efforts in that direction.

His military ability at length won him one post after another, with gradual promotions in rank (including the coveted one to *paşa*, or general) following the victories of his forces in North Africa, in the Balkans, on the Gallipoli Peninsula, and on the Russian front, as well as in a crucial holding action on the Syrian front. In all of these military actions, Mustafa Kemal had demonstrated both his clear-headed judgment and his ability to lead his troops to victory against unbelievably heavy odds. Moreover, he had unmasked Enver Paşa's shortsightedness in aligning the interests of Ottoman Turkey with those of Germany in World War I, an alignment that Mustafa Kemal had opposed from the outset. With the defeat of the British on the Syrian front and the subsequent signing of the British-Turkish Armistice, Enver Paşa and his two colleagues, Cemal Paşa and Talat Paşa — the ruling triumvirate of the Committee for Union and Progress — fled into exile, and Mustafa Kemal was thus free to enter perhaps the most important phase of his service to Turkey: the foundation of the ideal and the instruments for a *republic* of Turkey as a Westward-looking and revitalized nation. A lapse in Ottoman judgment, curiously, set the stage for this phase. Under pressure from the Allies, then occupying Istanbul, to curb the lawlessness in Anatolia (formerly called Asia Minor) following the close of World War I, Damad Ferid, the new sultan Vahideddin's Grand Vizier, yielded to an adviser's suggestion that Mustafa Kemal be posted to this unpleasant assignment; the young military officer, then in Istanbul, had proved irritating with his outspoken criticism of Ottoman policies, and his absence from Allied-occupied Istanbul would be welcomed by those already chafing at the Allies' presence. With slight misgivings, Damad Ferid sealed and then signed Mustafa Kemal's orders to Samsun, in Anatolia, to disarm and restore order among the unruly peasants, bandits, and demobilized servicemen in that area. His misgivings were better founded than he could have anticipated: far from repressing the nationalistic sentiments and behavior of these rural Turkish patriots, Mustafa Kemal undertook at once (he landed at Samsun on May 19, 1919) to encourage and direct them.

Acutely aware that if Turkey were to survive as a nation, its leadership and its strength must come from the Anatolian people themselves rather than from a revival of the corrupt and cowed Ottoman line, Mustafa Kemal and three of his long-time colleagues — Ali Fuad (later surnamed Cebesoy), Refet (later surnamed Bele), and Rauf (later surnamed Orbay) — led in the formation of a Nationalist government centered in Anatolia, well removed from Istanbul (Constantinople), the old stronghold of the Turkish Sultanate and the seat of the toppled Ottoman Empire. After several preliminary meetings (the most important one a National Congress at Sivas in September 1919 urged by Mustafa Kemal), the Turkish Grand National Assembly was convened in April 1920 in central Anatolia at Angora (Ankara), and Mustafa Kemal was elected its president. Shortly thereafter, the Ottoman government, already having yielded to the humiliating conditions imposed upon Turkey by the Allies, took strong notice of this challenge to what remained of its traditional authority: an Istanbul tribunal issued death sentences for seven Nationalist leaders, including Mustafa Kemal, the first step in what would prove to be a civil war between the old Turkey, represented by the Istanbul government, and the new Turkey, represented by the Nationalist government centered in Ankara.

The Nationalist group had few troops at its command, but these troops were supported in their defense of the Ankara government by guerrilla bands under Nationalist direction. They managed by adroit leadership to hold the key cities in Anatolia for the Nationalists, despite the efforts of the Sultan's troops to dislodge them. In the midst of this struggle for the support and preservation of the Nationalist cause, word came of the terms of the Treaty of Sèvres, the treaty the Allies imposed in 1920 on the Ottoman Empire at the close of World War I. The unfair terms of this treaty, signed by the Sultan's representative, so enraged the Turks that the treaty proved the deciding factor in winning support for the Nationalist movement. By acceding to the dismemberment of all but a small portion of landlocked Anatolia among the British, the Greeks, the French, and the Italians and by agreeing to the establishment of an independent Armenia and an autonomous Kurdistan, the Sultanate had clearly sold out to the enemy and no longer deserved the support of the Turkish nation. From now on, the interests of Turkey and its possibilities for survival lay with the Nationalists under the leadership of Mustafa Kemal.

Mustafa Kemal, undefeated in pitched battle, sure of himself, a master of tactics, was convinced that, given adequate powers by the Grand National Assembly, he could lead the aroused Turks to victory against the Allies' attempts to dismember Turkey and thus could save his nation for its people. For three months, he said, he would need absolute power in the name of the Assembly. For that short period, he would be no less than a military dictator. After considerable debate, the Assembly granted him the power he asked. (The three-month grant of power was renewed by the Assembly repeatedly as each term expired, always to meet an acknowledged need or emergency.)

To commit Turkey's civilians to an all-out war effort, he levied a tax on them: each family must provide a pair of shoes, a pair of socks, and a packet of underwear. In addition, he demanded all arms and ammunition (including the military supplies salvaged under his direction from Turkey's enemies) and a portion of all beasts of burden — oxen, horses, donkeys, and camels.

From businesses he demanded raw materials; from producers, food. Women were put to work on the farms and with the long ox-drawn military supply wagon trains. Every available man was taken into the armed forces. Thus every sector of the Turkish economy and the Turkish population was committed to this war for survival.

Although the Nationalists were outnumbered, they had the soundest possible reason for dedicated fighting: they were defending their homeland. In this desperate and seemingly hopeless fight against all odds, Mustafa Kemal — strongly aided by İsmet Bey (later surnamed İnönü because of his remarkable victories at İnönü) — reached his crowning military achievement: the post-World-War-I defeat of the combined forces of Great Britain, France, Italy, and Greece by his raggle-taggle guerrilla Nationalist army. Following the crushing defeat of the Greek forces in 1921, Mustafa Kemal was awarded by the grateful Grand National Assembly the title of *Gazi* ("war hero"). Under his leadership, Turkey — long labeled "the sick man of Europe" — had proved itself a nation with a dream of its own, and with determination to see that dream brought to reality. At last, Mustafa Kemal was everywhere hailed as the conquering hero, a new breed of leader for this new nation.

Ahead of Turkey now lay a decision: Should Turkey, thus miraculously spared degradation and dismemberment, follow up her military victory with an attack across the Straits of the Dardanelles, attempting to take by force from Great Britain that strategic bit of land that might conceivably be won by negotiation? Or should Turkey avoid this dangerous step toward a renewal of the world war, and, participating as a victor, settle her claims at the conference table? To the obvious relief of the Allies, Mustafa Kemal chose the second alternative, wisely determining Turkey's "own soil" as Anatolia and that precious toehold on eastern Thrace and the Straits of the Dardanelles, territory that could be comfortably governed. In this way, both Great Britain and Turkey could withdraw from the threatened conflict with dignity. At the Conference (in Mudanya) it was agreed that Turkey was to have eastern Thrace and the Straits, the territory she would have sought by military means had Mustafa Kemal chosen the first alternative instead of the second; subsequent international agreements confirming Turkey's intention to limit her territorial ambitions to the lines she had indicated assured all nations that Turkey intended to keep the peace. Other terms equally favorable to Turkey were agreed upon at the Conference, and the armistice agreement was signed on October 11, 1922, by the representatives of Great Britain, France, Italy, Greece, and Nationalist Turkey. Now all that lay ahead was the Peace Conference in Lausanne, at which the Nationalist government was to be represented by İsmet Bey (İnönü), a staunch supporter of Mustafa Kemal in his plans for the new nation.

When the Allies invited a representative of the Sultanate also to represent Turkey, the members of the Grand National Assembly were enraged. This was exactly the right moment, Mustafa Kemal decided, for the abolition of the Sultanate. He drafted a proposal separating the Sultanate (temporal power) from the Caliphate (religious power) and abolishing the Sultanate forever; the Caliphate was to be awarded to the most appropriate member of the Ottoman dynasty. By well-timed arguments and by speeches in committee, he secured acceptance of the proposal; its adoption by the Grand National Assembly was achieved by his adroit presentation. Thus the rule of Turkey by the Sultan was ended, and the rule of this victorious young nation by its own people was firmly established.

There followed the first genuine political campaign

in the Middle East. Mustafa Kemal organized the People's Party (later called the Republican People's Party), dedicated to the goal of Westernizing Turkey and bringing it forward as a progressive nation. In one town and village after the other, Mustafa Kemal spoke to the people of his plans, confident of their support for his leadership. A measure of resistance to the *Gazi*'s continued domination of the Nationalists became apparent in the resignations of two of Mustafa Kemal's closest friends, Ali Fuad (Cebesoy) and Rauf (Orbay), from their positions with the Nationalist government; they were disturbed because Mustafa Kemal had not laid aside his position as the ultimate arbiter in the affairs of the country to make room for a truly democratic government, a rule not by one powerful person — no matter how talented — but by the people themselves. (Able replacements for these two were found in Fethi [later surnamed Okyar] and in İsmet [İnönü].) But Mustafa Kemal sensed that the Turkish people were not yet ready for a Western-type democracy; much needed to be done educationally and economically, he felt, before the average Turkish citizen could effectively determine his own best interests. Resolved to do all in his power to turn the faces of his people toward the West and to prepare them in every way possible for a real democracy in Turkey, he ensured that the capital of the new nation would be located in the heart of Turkey, from which had come the means of her salvation. Despite the protests of many newsmen and the intelligentsia of Istanbul, Ankara was decided upon by the Grand National Assembly as the new capital. Then little more than a village on the semiarid central Anatolian plateau, Ankara nevertheless represented the new Turkish temperament and the Turkish will to survive as a nation. And "Istanbul," for hundreds of years the name given by the Turks to the city that Westerners called Constan-

89

tinople, was to be the official name of that storied city on the Bosphorus, a city deliberately divested of Turkish political and intellectual leadership.

The republic that Mustafa Kemal envisioned was a totally new form of government in the Middle East, one that even the new Assembly, composed of men whom the Gazi himself had largely chosen, would find it difficult to reconcile with their ideas of what was appropriate for a Moslem nation. Very well, then: he himself would see it through. With İsmet's (İnönü's) cooperation, he drafted changes in the Constitution adopted by the Grand National Assembly in 1921 to include, among others, this major clause: "The form of the government of the Turkish state is a Republic." The President of the Republic was to be elected by the Grand National Assembly; the President would appoint a Prime Minister, who in turn would appoint the members of his Cabinet, with the approval of the Assembly. The revised Constitution was then submitted to Mustafa Kemal's political party, the People's Party, for adoption. Mustafa Kemal spoke briefly to the leaders of the party, explaining the reasoning behind the changes, and despite some protest the new Constitution was approved. It was also accepted in short order by the Assembly, though many had misgivings about it because they had had little or no acquaintance with any democratic form of government. Mustafa Kemal was duly elected President, and the new Republic was officially proclaimed on October 29, 1923. The man who had so long sought to be his country's leader was in fact now recognized as exactly that.

Since Mustafa Kemal saw a decided threat to the new Republic in the Caliphate, a link with the Ottoman past and a competitive government structure, he set about to have it legally abolished. The old religious schools (of the Hafız Mehmet type) were transformed into secular schools, and the old religious courts gave way to a legal code based on that of Switzerland. The Moslem faith was not abolished; instead, the Turks were declared free to worship as they saw fit.

Reforms undertaken by the new Republic under Mustafa Kemal's determined leadership ranged from a change in hats (from the Ottoman-Moslem fez — outlawed on November 25, 1925 — to a head-covering with a brim), through the unveiling and emancipation of women (including the abolition of polygamy), to the substitution of a Latin alphabet for the traditional Arabic script. Unrelated as these reforms may seem, they all represented giant steps toward the Westernizing of Turkey, the goal set by the Nationalists and faithfully achieved in their dramatic departure from the old image of the Turkish Empire.

Of all these reforms, undoubtedly the most central was that of the alphabet. Mustafa Kemal here showed his natural bent as a teacher: once the new alphabet had been developed, he himself undertook with blackboard and chalk to teach it to the people; he became in effect the schoolteacher of the whole nation. Not only had the timetable for the Language Committee's preparation of the required alphabet been greatly accelerated, but the President of the Republic had decreed that three months from the date on which he had announced the new alphabet at a public gathering (August 9, 1928) all the newspapers, all the street signs, all written Turkish would appear in the new letters. Every man, woman, and child was urged to learn the new alphabet and to teach it to others. Once the letters had been learned, reading and writing would follow comfortably, since the new alphabet was perfectly phonetic: each letter had a single sound, and the sounds represented by the letters were precisely those sounds found in spoken Turkish. Mustafa Kemal proved to be a most effective teacher indeed, for the new alphabet spread rapidly, and a modern education was thus brought within the finger-tips of each Turk.

As soon as the new script — called the Turkish script, to distinguish it from the Arabic — was made law, in November 1928, a formal examination was set up to test the citizens' knowledge of it. Within the first year, more than a million of the thirteen million Turkish citizens had passed the test and were the proud holders of a diploma saying so. Of course, young people learned the new script readily; they became the teachers of their elders. The new alphabet accomplished one significant aim in addition to opening up the Western world to Turkish readers: it effectively closed the door on the old Ottoman world, and on the literature of the Moslem faith and on Ottoman history, for those records were available not in the Turkish script but in Arabic, a script unintelligible to most Turks. In a very real sense, the only direction now in which the Turks could look was forward.

Two other changes under Mustafa Kemal's leader-ship were significant in bringing Turkey into step with the Western nations: the change in measurement of time in terms of clocks and calendars and the matter of providing every Turk with a surname. As for the former, the old Turkish system of keying time to the hours of prayer and of dating events in terms of Moslem history gave way in 1926 to the Western Gregorian calendar and the international twenty-four-hour clock; along with these changes, the holy day, or Sabbath, was designated as Sunday rather than Friday. The matter of surnames was handled in a most ingenious fashion: By January 1, 1935, every Turk was required by the National Assembly to have a surname. The choice of a surname rested with the father of the family; the name selected would be a permanent one, inherited by the children in Western fashion. To assist those who could not decide on an appropriate surname, Mustafa Kemal had the newspapers publish lists of names — thousands of names. All earlier titles (including Mustafa Kemal's own *Gazi*) were declared abolished; Mustafa Kemal himself received his surname *Atatürk* (Father of the Turks, or Father-Turk) from the National Assembly. His was an appropriate name indeed, for he had given the Turk reason to be proud of his home and his heritage, and made him ready to take his place on the twentieth-century stage of history. In truth, just as the child Mustafa had set those two goldfinches free, the man Mustafa Kemal Atatürk had set his own people free — free from the past, free from the dictates of other political powers, free to walk tall among the nations of the world — free to *sing*.

Two distinguishing features marked Kemal Atatürk as a radical departure from those would-be dictators then arising in other parts of the world, and both of those features are related to his personal view of his country. First, he saw Turkey not as a claimant to empire but as a single nation within definite geographical boundaries that might rightly be called hers. He sought for Turkey not an increasing power over other nations, but a power over her own homogeneous people, sharers of the same traits and traditions and culture. Second, he saw Turkey as a nation eventually able, though in this time ruled by one man, one day to rule herself democratically, to go on without him, side by side with other modern democratic nations in a modern world. He had both vision and force; either without the other would have caused him to fall short of the goal.

In the attainment of his high station, Atatürk revealed touches both of the boy on the farm at Rapla and of the determined individual who found his own niche as an eager military student. He established a farm of his own near Ankara where various agricultural experiments are still being undertaken. His love of trees and other growing things is still evidenced in the parks and treed thoroughfares of the capital city; his affection for dogs continued to the end. His interests in writing, in reading, and in debate developed during his student years persisted, and accounted in considerable measure for his ability to inspire, to enlighten, and to persuade his people. His strong will, marked from the very beginning, was no small factor in the achievement of his monumental goals for his nation. Yes, indeed, this boy *was* father of this man.

Atatürk had, as a soldier, a patriot, and a statesman, served his people well. Despite the inroads of illness (two heart attacks and the development of a liver ailment), he survived to see the accomplishment of his aims for his people. But late in 1937, his magnificent physique began to give way before the burdens that a perpetually active life had placed upon it. Despite pain and weariness, he continued to keep a demanding routine until he was no longer able to leave his bed. Still, from his bedside he continued to direct the affairs of Turkey until his death, on November 10, 1938.

Announcement of his death stunned the Turkish nation. Perhaps the government bulletin issued on the occasion of his death expresses best how those who loved the nation saw him:

"The Turkish fatherland has lost its great builder, the Turkish nation its mighty leader, mankind a great son."

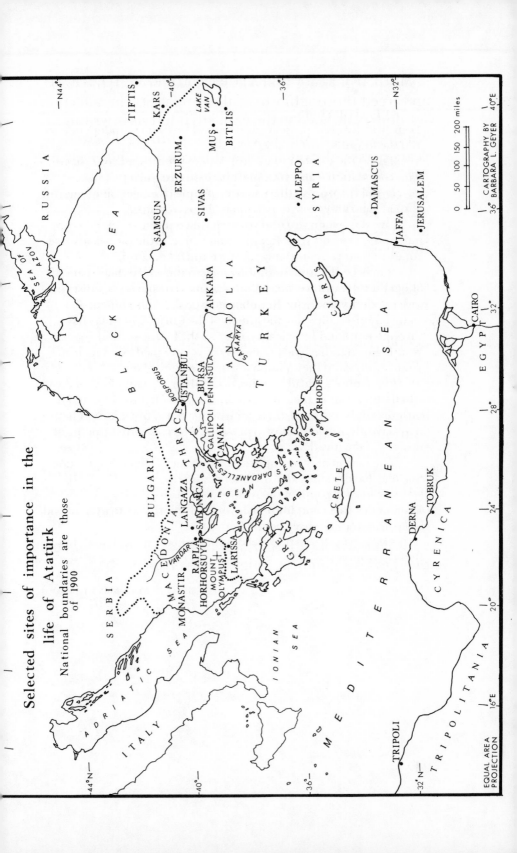

Selected sites of importance in the life of Atatürk

National boundaries are those of 1900

CARTOGRAPHY BY
BARBARA L. GEYER

0   50   100   150   200 miles

EQUAL AREA
PROJECTION

RUSSIA

SEA OF AZOV

BLACK SEA

TIFLIS

KARS

LAKE VAN

ERZURUM

SAMSUN

MUŞ

BITLIS

SIVAS

ANKARA

ALEPPO

SYRIA

DAMASCUS

JERUSALEM

JAFFA

SERBIA

BULGARIA

MACEDONIA

VARDAR

MONASTIR

HORHORSUYU

RAPLA

MOUNT OLYMPUS

LARISSA

LANGAZA

SALONICA

THRACE

ISTANBUL

BOSPORUS

BURSA

GALLIPOLI PENINSULA

ÇANAK

DARDANELLES

SAKARYA

ANATOLIA

TURKEY

CYPRUS

EGYPT

CAIRO

GREECE

AEGEAN SEA

CRETE

RHODES

ADRIATIC SEA

ITALY

IONIAN SEA

MEDITERRANEAN SEA

TRIPOLI

TRIPOLITANIA

CYRENICA

DERNA

TOBRUK

N44°

—40°

—36°

N32°

40°E

36°

32°

28°

24°

20°

16°E

44°N

40°

36°

32°N

MUSTAFA KEMAL ATATÜRK'S ADDRESS TO YOUTH

O Turkish Youth!
Your first duty is to preserve and defend forever the independence and the Republic of Turkey.

This is the sole foundation of your existence and your future. This foundation is also your most precious treasure.

In the future also there may be people of malice, at home and abroad, who may try to deprive you of this treasure.

One day, when you find yourself called upon to defend your independence and your Republic, tarry not, in the face of adverse conditions and circumstances, before you take action.

It may be that the conditions and circumstances may seem altogether too unfavorable! Your enemies conspiring against your independence and your Republic may be the embodiment of victories unparalleled in the annals of the world. They may have, through craft and force, taken over all the fortresses and arsenals of your beloved fatherland. They may have occupied every inch of your country and they may have dispersed her armies.

Even more painful and disastrous than all, it may be that those who hold power in the country may have fallen into error and be misguided. Worst of all, these men may actually be traitors. They may have identified their own personal interests with the political designs of the invaders.

The nation may be impoverished to the point of desperation. She may have totally exhausted her resources.

O Turkish Youth of the future!
Even under these conditions it is your foremost duty to uphold and save the independence and the Republic of Turkey.

The strength you may need is there, in the noble blood that flows in your veins!

[TRANSLATION BY GÜNSELİ TAMKOÇ]

96